Grade 5

Written by Robyn Silbey
Illustrated by Ann Stein

FS-23205 Math Made Simple Grade 5

23740 Hawthorne Blvd.
Torrance, CA 90505

Introduction

Math plays a vital role in everyone's life on a daily basis—in a variety of situations. It is, therefore, absolutely a necessity that children develop, understand, and learn to apply math skills.

What is an integer?

How will math make me better understand sports? cooking? shopping?

How are decimals and fractions related?

How is volume different from area?

These and other questions are children's attempts to make sense of mathematics concepts.

Math Made Simple has been designed to help students develop a basic understanding of math concepts and to help them practice skills and algorithms related to those concepts. The activities presented in this book help students learn to apply these skills and concepts in a variety of problem solving situations.

The objective of *Math Made Simple* is to help all students succeed in math. In order to ensure success for all learners, the activities in this book are presented in a variety of formats.

The book is divided into five sections. In the front of each section are Teacher Resource pages. These pages feature many exciting extension activities that you can guide the students to do. Another fascinating aspect of the Teacher Resource pages is the School-Home Connection activities. These activities provide a great way for students to apply the skills and concepts presented to situations at home. These kinds of activities are a great way to show students and their families that opportunities for learning math can arise at home as well as at school and that learning math can be interesting, fun, and valuable.

Behind the Teacher Resource pages are a lot of fun and stimulating activity pages students can complete to learn the important math skills and concepts featured in the section. The activities include decoding messages, solving riddles, working puzzles, coloring, and much more. These activities provide yet another exciting means for students to better understand the concepts and skills presented in each section.

The concepts covered in *Math Made Simple* are basic to most grade 5 mathematics programs. Students will develop conceptual understanding of and will practice skills relating to the following categories: addition and subtraction of whole numbers and decimals; multiplication and division of whole numbers and decimals; understanding fractions and mixed numbers; adding, subtracting, multiplying, and dividing fractions and mixed numbers; ratios and percents; geometry; and perimeter, area, and volume.

To reinforce the math topics presented in this book and to help students gain a greater understanding of these topics, prepare (or have the students prepare) math journals. These provide students with places to write down the thinking processes or steps that they have used to solve problems. They are also wonderful places for students to record any interesting mathematical discoveries they make. Let the students share their journals with each other and with you when applicable.

Another valuable tool you and the students can make are erasable cards (i.e., laminated pieces of paper). These are great for students to use when doing group activities. Students can write down answers to problems using crayons and hold them up. This enables you to quickly check to see who understands the concept being presented. Smaller groups can then be created to reteach a particular skill.

Regardless of your reasons for implementing *Math Made Simple*, you will be delighted as you watch your students discover how interesting and fun learning math can be!

Whole Numbers and Decimals

Students will benefit greatly from the whole number and decimal reinforcement and extension ideas described in this section (pages 1–25). Be sure to provide students with ample opportunities to work with manipulatives and complete several examples with your guidance. Also provide students with time for conceptual understanding before proceeding through the more independent student activity pages.

Be sure to point out to students how they can use their new skills in everyday life. For example, students can use their knowledge of whole numbers and decimals as they compare heights and distances or compute batting averages. Help students observe the world around them and identify their own connections to whole numbers and decimals.

CONCEPTS

The ideas and activities presented in this section will help students explore the following concepts:

- *adding whole numbers and decimals*
- *subtracting whole numbers and decimals*
- *multiplying whole numbers and decimals*
- *dividing whole numbers and decimals*
- *the distributive property*
- *problem solving*
- *finding averages*

Adding and Subtracting Whole Numbers and Decimals

DECIMAL DISCOVERIES WITH BASE TEN BLOCKS

Class Activity

Give students base ten manipulatives. Explain to students that a block represents one whole, or 1.0; a long block represents one tenth, or 0.1; and a unit block represents one hundredth, or 0.01. Show students how ten unit blocks equal one long block, etc. (This really helps visual students to better understand decimals.) Allow students time to model numbers such as 0.8, 0.02, 0.73, and 1.25. Students should be able to write and say each number they model using manipulatives. Next, have students use the manipulatives to find sums and differences. For example, students may use the manipulatives to find the sum of 1.32 + 0.48 (1.8) or the difference of 1.3 – 0.49 (0.81).

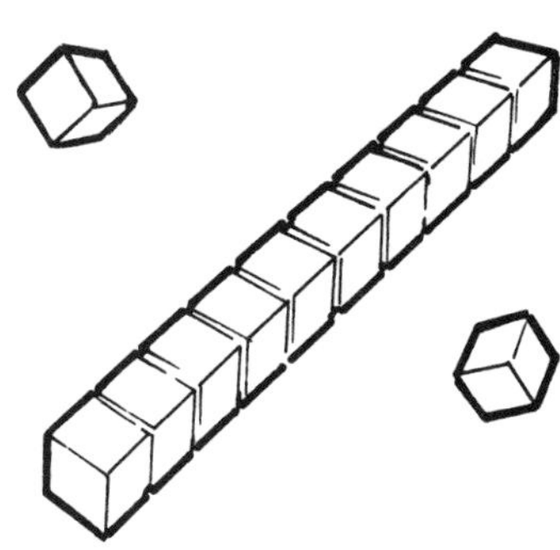

WRITING DECIMAL NUMBERS

Manipulative Activity

Have each student write a decimal to the nearest hundredth. Each decimal should be less than 10. Then have students work in pairs to do the following: (1) share decimals and use place value blocks to add them, recording their work using symbols; (2) determine which decimal is greater; (3) use place value blocks to model the greater decimal, then subtract the lesser decimal. Again, students should record their work using symbols.

DECIMAL DILEMMAS

Writing Activities

Writing About Decimals

In their journals, have students write all the steps they would follow to do the following:

a. Find the sum of 4.367, 2.08, and 3.6. (10.047)
b. Find the difference of 4 and 2.94. (1.06)

Have students exchange papers and follow each other's directions for solving the problems.

Estimated Sums and Differences

Have students write three different problems that each have a sum of 10.5 and three that have a difference of 0.5. Ask students to describe how they found their answers. Then have each student trade his or her paper with a partner and check each other's problems.

ESTIMATING WITH DECIMALS

Writing Activity

In their journals, have students write their own directions for the following: (1) rounding numbers to the nearest tenth and to the nearest hundredth, (2) rounding sums, and (3) rounding differences. Then have students use their directions to solve the problems on one of the activity pages in this section or in another independent assignment of your choice.

Homework

Decimals and Money

Provide students with menus from fast-food eateries or other restaurants. Have students "order" a meal of their choice and calculate the cost. They could also find the difference between the cost of two entrees, desserts, or appetizers. You could also have students work in pairs so that they can compare the costs of their meals. Display the menus and students' work on a bulletin board.

DECIMAL GLOSSARY

Writing Activity

In their journals, have students construct an illustrated glossary containing terms such as the following: *whole number, decimal, tenth, hundredth, thousandth, regrouping, rounding, estimating, sum,* and *difference.* Let students use their glossaries as references as they work through activities and reproducibles.

TIME CONNECTION

Homework

Have students record the number of minutes they spend on their homework in a five-day period. Challenge them to find the total amount of time spent. You may need to remind students to regroup 60 minutes for 1 hour.

Homework

School-Home Connection

Health Connection

Have each student list the items that he or she thinks would make a healthy dinner. Then have the students refer to each ingredient's packaging or a nutrition book to estimate the total number of grams of sodium or grams of fat in the meal. Have each student decide with his or her family if the meal is actually healthy in regard to sodium and fat.

Miles per Gallon

Have students record the mileage from the odometer of one of their families' cars right after the gas tank has been filled. When the gas tank is filled again, they should record the new number shown on the odometer. Students should then calculate the number of miles (to the nearest tenth of a mile) driven on that tank of gas. Have students do this for five fill-ups and determine an "average" distance per tank of gas. As a class, compare each type of car and the average number of miles per tank of gas. Put the comparisons on a bulletin board.

EXACT OR ESTIMATE?

Class Activity

Brainstorm with your students to create lists of when an exact answer is needed and when it is more appropriate to have an estimate. Then give students situations and ask them to analyze the situations to determine whether they need an estimate or an exact answer. A possible situation could be as follows: *You are making programs for a school show. You ask how many tickets have been sold. Do you need an exact amount or an estimate?*

NUMBER FUN

Class Activities

Guess and Check Riddles

Have students solve some "Guess and Check" riddles. (See the example to the right.) Discuss solution strategies as a class. Then have students make up their own "Guess and Check" riddles to try on classmates.

What two numbers have a sum of 113 and a difference of 13? (63 and 50)

Mystery Number

Write the following riddle on the overhead or chalkboard: *I am a three-digit number. All my digits are even, and their sum is 12. My digits are all different, and they are in order from greatest to least. What number could I be?* (Possible: 642 or 840) Have students explain how they used the clues to find their answers. Then challenge students to make up riddles for their classmates to solve.

Name ____________________

Secret Word

"Just About" Answers

Use rounding to estimate each sum or difference below. Then shade a section in the box at the bottom of the page that matches your answer to find a secret word.

A.

28 + 92 = 120	73 + 68	133 − 67	166 − 78	617 + 376

B.

44 + 59	1,486 − 626	681 − 324	6,790 + 3,456	15,897 − 8,584

C.

368 + 429	1,295 − 787	1,869 − 451	1,303 − 698	17,498 − 8,329

D.

12,645 − 9,103	698 − 462	2,375 + 2,814	1,014 + 5,321	8,247 + 9,983

120	7,000	400	3,000	1,000	19,000	
4,000	300	140	8,000	1,400	9,000	15,000
800	700	5,000	11,000	18,000	14,000	17,000
200	2,000	90	12,000	6,000	10,000	20,000
600	60	500	16,000	100	13,000	900

What's the secret word? ____________

Name________________________________

Riddle

Talk With the Animals

Add or subtract. Use your answers to write and solve a riddle.

O. 5,038 + 2,847

W. 6,034 − 2,993

N. 7,645 + 8,397

C. 57,634 + 18,906

D. 9,634 − 5,798

E. 3,497 + 867

K. 4,263 − 1,896

H. 9,156 + 8,375

P. 54,375 − 36,693

L. 3,073 − 897

U. 5,372 − 439

A. 23,842 − 1,632

S. 32,693 + 41,221

I. 14,734 − 2,961

F. 1,646 + 1,826 = _______ G. 9,874 − 8,887 = _______ T. 4,419 + 2,987 = _______

___ 3,041 ___ 17,531 ___ 22,210 ___ 7,406   ___ 3,836 ___ 7,885 ___ 4,364 ___ 73,914   ___ 22,210

___ 76,540 ___ 17,531 ___ 11,773 ___ 76,540 ___ 2,367 ___ 4,364 ___ 16,042   ___ 73,914 ___ 17,682 ___ 4,364 ___ 22,210 ___ 2,367 ?

___ 3,472 ___ 7,885 ___ 3,041 ___ 2,176   ___ 2,176 ___ 22,210 ___ 16,042 ___ 987 ___ 4,993 ___ 22,210 ___ 987 ___ 4,364

Name____

Make a Million

Complete each problem so that the sum is one million.

A.

237,512	456,897	79,936	________
+ ________	+ ________	+ ________	+ 384,207
1,000,000	1,000,000	1,000,000	1,000,000

B.

564,216	935,142	________	499,999
+ ________	+ ________	+ 99,384	+ ________
1,000,000	1,000,000	1,000,000	1,000,000

C.

424,116	________	82,936	496,385
________	384,109	426,817	________
+ 61,532	+ 123,816	+ ________	+ 216,419
1,000,000	1,000,000	1,000,000	1,000,000

D.

369,804	________	831,678	23,182
________	664,819	________	976,596
+ 566,157	+ 309,662	+ 29,814	+ ________
1,000,000	1,000,000	1,000,000	1,000,000

Write two problems of your own that have sums of one million.

E.

____
+ ________
1,000,000

F.

____
+ ________
1,000,000

Name ____________________

What's Missing?

Find the missing numbers.

D. 7.93 + 1.08 − 3.09 + = 8.62

E. 5.35 − 1.16 + − 0.61 = 13.4

F. 12.24 − + 5.2 − 3.9 = 5.38

G. 3.46 + 8.7 + − 3.7 = 18.46

H. 48.9 − 24.25 + 16.1 − 0.4 =

I. + 17.46 − 4.7 + 8.02 = 32.89

Name ______________________________

Dino-Mite Decimals

Add or subtract.

A.

2.9	8.09	12.8
+ 7.9	+ 2.66	− 7.6

B.

12.95	7.05	147.34
+ 13.67	− 3.06	− 29.61

C. 9.16 − 4.31   6.75 − 1.2   8 − 3.78

D.

347.2	7.406	125.7	275.3	7.7
− 182.6	− 2.987	+ 32.98	− 199.9	+ 33.5

E.

1.106	0.871	4.92	25.9	2.96
+ 5.926	− 0.682	− 0.98	+ 106.7	+ 2.04

F.

30.173	10.61	52.8	708.25	3.786
− 18.92	− 1.96	− 22.09	+ 95.17	+ 0.374

G. 32.6 + 1.97   8.03 − 5.66   14.521 + 7.498   42.53 + 0.96

Name ______________________________

Name That Meal

The Wootton cheerleaders went to Anchor Inn after the big game. Use the Anchor Inn menu below to solve the problems.

1. Rochelle ordered soup and broiled fish. Was $10.00 enough to cover her meal? Explain.

____

2. Harvey had $12 to spend. He ordered broiled fish and a soft drink. Does he have enough money left for dessert? If so, what might he order?

____

3. Angela ordered salad and a dessert. She spent about $6. Which dessert did Angela order?

____

4. Thomas ordered an appetizer, shrimp, a fruit cup, and a drink. He spent about $20. What appetizer and drink did Thomas order?

____

5. Wilma spent about $5 less than Thomas. She ordered an appetizer, shrimp, ice cream, and juice. What appetizer did Wilma order?

____

6. Choose your own appetizer, main dish, drink, and dessert. Estimate your total cost.

____

Multiplying and Dividing Whole Numbers and Decimals

PRODUCTS WITH 99

Learning Activity

Show students how to use mental math to find the product of any number and 99. Tell them to simply multiply the number by 100, then subtract the original number.

For example: 5 x 99 = (5 x 100) – 5 = 495

Have students use the "99 method" to find the following products:

a. 7 x 99 (693) b. 30 x 99 (2,970) c. 25 x 99 (2,475)

d. 45 x 99 (4,455) e. 95 x 99 (9,405) f. 100 x 99 (9,900)

ESTIMATING DECIMAL PRODUCTS

Learning Activity

Some students experience difficulty with the placement of decimal points in products involving decimals. Suggest that students round each decimal to the nearest whole number or to the nearest ten, then multiply. Tell students that they can use this estimated product to help them check the decimal point placement in the actual product. For example: 4.87 x 8.16 is about 5 x 8, or about 40. The digits that make up the actual answer are 397392. Using the estimated product of 40, students can place the decimal to show a product of 39.7392.

Writing Activity

FIND THE QUOTIENT

In their journals, have students write a detailed explanation of how they would find the quotient of 96,743 ÷ 38. Students should include how they estimated each of the quotient digits; whether they were too large, too small, or just right; how they adjusted their estimates when needed; and so on. (Quotient = 2,545 R33)

PRODUCT PROBLEMS

Class Activities

Products in Time

Have students find each product below. Then students should order the answers from smallest to largest. (1) number of seconds in one day (86,400); (2) number of minutes in one year (525,600); (3) number of hours in a century (876,000) (Order: 86,400; 525,600; 876,000)

Odd Jobs

Have students estimate such things as the number of hours per week that they might babysit or the number of homes to which they might deliver newspapers. Tell students to imagine that they are paid $3.50 per hour to babysit, and they are paid $0.07 for each newspaper they deliver. Have students calculate their possible earnings per week, per month, and per year.

RISING TO NEW HEIGHTS

Group Activities

Class Heights

Have pairs of students measure each other's height in centimeters using a meter stick or metric tape measure. Have students record their heights on a chart using the following headings:

Students' Names Height (cm) Height (m)

Have students describe how they used the heights in centimeters to calculate the heights in meters (multiplied each measure by 100).

Average Height

Help students find their heights in inches or in centimeters. Have students record their heights on the board. Then discuss with students how they could find the average height for students in the class. Finally, have students find the average height for the class. You may wish to have students use calculators to help them.

CALCULATOR NUMBER SENSE

Game

Have students play this game with partners. Each player needs a calculator. Each player starts by entering 14 into a calculator. Then the players multiply 14 by five different numbers using any numbers or decimals of their choice. The goal is to reach 150 in six tries. The player with the product closest to 150 scores one point. Then students start a new game by choosing new numbers and a new goal. The first player to reach five points wins the match.

Class Activity

Grocery Shopping

Bring in and display a large grocery store advertisement. Have students record the price per pound of two types of meat and two kinds of cheese. Tell students to imagine that they need to buy 2.5 pounds of each item. Ask students to do the following: determine whether $20 will be enough to buy everything, estimate the total cost, and find the actual total cost.

USING NUMBER SENSE TO ESTIMATE QUOTIENTS

Game

Have each student work with a partner. Students agree on a three-digit target quotient, such as 345. Partners take turns calling out any six digits from 0 through 9. Each student records the numbers on his or her paper. Each student uses the six digits to form a division problem having a 2-digit divisor and a 4-digit dividend. Students find the quotients of their problems, then determine which quotient is closer to the target number. The student whose quotient is closer to the target number wins a point. Students may choose a new target number and play a new round. Play continues until one student wins 5 points.

Manipulative Activity

MULTIPLYING DECIMALS WITH PLACE VALUE GRIDS

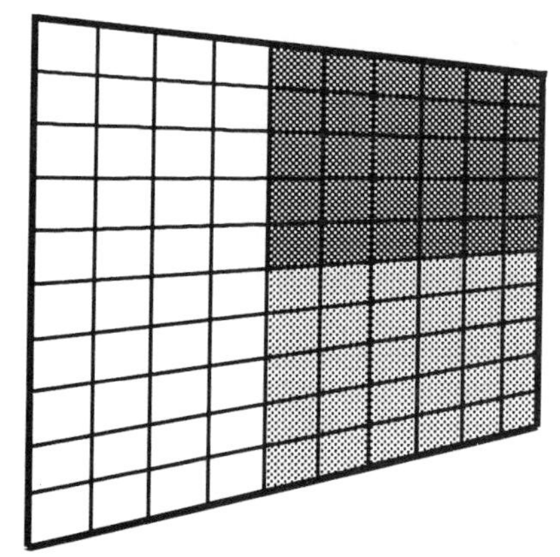

Distribute copies of decimal grids (10 by 10) to students. Make sure students understand that the square represents one whole. Have students find the product of 0.6 x 0.5 by highlighting 6 tenths (strips or rows) of the decimal square and by shading 5 tenths of the highlighted region (half of the highlighted region). Students will find that the product is 30 hundredths, or 0.3. Provide students with more practice on the grid paper by giving them such problems as 0.3 x 0.4 (0.12), 0.8 x 0.7 (0.56), and 0.5 x 0.4 (0.2).

WORD PROBLEM COLLECTION

Learning Center

Have students look in newspapers or magazines for three pictures which they can use to create division word problems. Have students cut out the pictures and write a problem beneath each one. Tell students to make sure that their problems can be solved and that each problem and quotient are reasonable. Then put the problems in a notebook for the students to take turns solving at their leisure.

DIVISIBILITY RULES

Class Activities

Dandy Divisibles

Have students list the first 15 multiples of 2, 5, and 10. Then challenge students to write their own rules for determining whether a number is divisible by 2, 5, or 10. Finally, have students make a list of five 3-digit numbers that are divisible by 2, divisible by 5, and divisible by 10. Make sure students understand that numbers that are divisible by 10 are also divisible by 2 and 5.

Small, but Big

Challenge students to find the smallest number that is divisible by all the numbers from 1 to 10. You may wish to tell students that the number has 4 digits. (2,520) Then ask students to find other numbers that can be divided evenly by all the numbers from 1 to 10. (These numbers include all the multiples of 2,520, such as 5,040; 10,080; and 20,160.)

COMPARISON SHOPPING

Class Activity

Have students cut out two pictures of the same products that their families often buy at the supermarket. For each picture, students should make a sale sign showing what it would cost to buy three or more product units (i.e., 3 for 99¢). Students should make sure that the price per unit is different for each product, and that it is exact, with no fractions of a cent remaining (no remainders). Next, have students determine the unit price for each item. Finally, they can compare unit prices for the products and determine which is the better buy.

BLOCK DIVISION

Manipulative Activity

Have students work in pairs to solve the problems below. One student finds the first quotient using place value blocks while his or her partner records the work on paper. Partners alternate roles as they work through the remaining problems.

a. 72 ÷ 4 (18) b. 84 ÷ 3 (28)
c. 346 ÷ 6 (57 R4) d. 212 ÷ 4 (53)
e. 486 ÷ 7 (69 R3) f. 644 ÷ 3 (214 R2)

RECIPES FOR ESTIMATED AND ACTUAL PRODUCTS

Group Activity

Have students write recipes for finding the estimated product and the actual product of 481 x 816 (400,000; 392,496). Allow students to read their recipes to partners, revise them, and write final drafts. Then have students use their recipes to find the estimated product and the actual product of 369 x 738 (280,000; 272,322).

DIVISION DESCRIPTIONS

Group Activity

Have students write a division problem for each description below. Have students select partners. Partners can solve and check each other's problems.

a. 1-digit divisor, 3-digit quotient, remainder of 7 (Ex: 999 ÷ 8 = 124 R7)

b. multiple of 10 divisor, 1-digit quotient, no remainder (Ex: 240 ÷ 60 = 4)

c. 2-digit divisor, 1-digit quotient, remainder of 5 (269 ÷ 44 = 6 R5)

Manipulative Activity

Dividing Decimals Using Money

Use play dollars, dimes, and pennies to help students understand the concept of dividing with decimals. Write problems on the board such as \$2.16 ÷ 2. Have students model the problem using 2 dollar bills, 1 dime, and 6 pennies. Students can separate the 2 dollar bills into two groups of \$1, then trade in the dime for 10 pennies, and separate the 16 pennies into two groups of 8. The quotient will be \$1.08. Repeat this procedure with several other examples.

PATTERNS WITH DECIMALS

Class Activity

Have students complete number patterns such as those shown below and explain how they found their answers. Students may use calculators to check their work.

7 x 54 (378)	7.03 x 4 (28.12)
0.7 x 54 (37.8)	7.03 x 0.4 (2.812)
0.07 x 54 (3.78)	7.03 x 0.04 (0.2812)
0.007 x 54 (0.378)	7.03 x 0.004 (0.02812)
0.0007 x 54 (0.0378)	7.03 x 0.0004 (0.002812)

SCHOOL-HOME CONNECTION

Homework

Fast-Food Figures

Have students save the receipts from meals at fast-food or other restaurants. They can divide the total amount spent by the number of people eating to find the average cost per person. It might be fun to have students keep a record of these for restaurant comparison purposes.

A Taxing Job

Have students find the tax charged on various items while shopping with their parents. For example, students may calculate the tax on a \$79.99 bicycle, given that the state tax is 5% (0.05). Parents may wish to have their child use a calculator to check his or her answers. This experience is especially helpful in students' understanding of consumer math education.

Name ______________________________

Riddle

Get Your Facts Straight

Complete each equation with a different factor pair. (Hint: Use multiplication facts to help you.)

A. 800

10 x 80

_____ x _____

_____ x _____

B. 1,000

_____ x _____

_____ x _____

_____ x _____

C. 1,500

_____ x _____

_____ x _____

_____ x _____

D. 1,200

_____ x _____

_____ x _____

_____ x _____

_____ x _____

E. 16,000

_____ x _____

_____ x _____

_____ x _____

_____ x _____

F. 20,000

_____ x _____

_____ x _____

_____ x _____

_____ x _____

G. 4,000

_____ x _____

_____ x _____

_____ x _____

_____ x _____

H. 240,000

_____ x _____

_____ x _____

_____ x _____

_____ x _____

Shade in the factors that you could NOT use. Then turn your paper so that the right side of the page is at the top. You will see what all of these numbers have in common.

10	40	70	90	70,000	700	30	200	90,000
30	300	700	20	700	60	70	40	9,000
80	500	900	60	9,000	50	400	90	9
7	90	7,000	900	90,000	100	10	20	7,000

Name____

Ring Around the Numbers

Circle two numbers in each box whose estimated product would be the amount shown.

A. Estimated Product: **200**

5	6
47	39

B. Estimated Product: **100**

49	9
25	2

C. Estimated Product: **300**

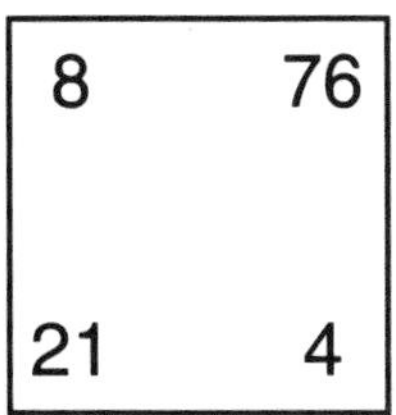

8	76
21	4

D. Estimated Product: **400**

12	23
19	85

E. Estimated Product: **800**

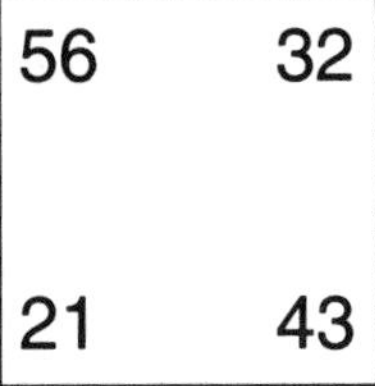

56	32
21	43

F. Estimated Product: **1,000**

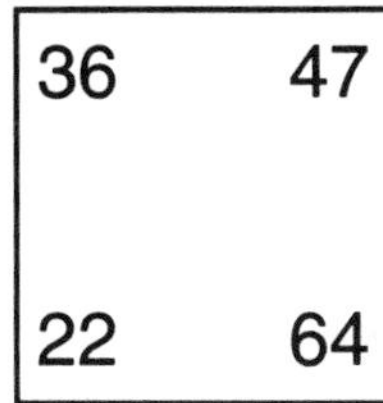

36	47
22	64

G. Estimated Product: **900**

31	12
45	29

H. Estimated Product: **1,200**

63	48
19	83

I. Estimated Product: **1,500**

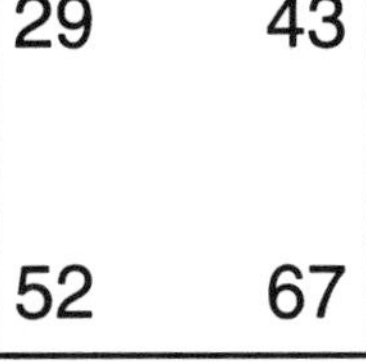

29	43
52	67

J. Estimated Product: **2,400**

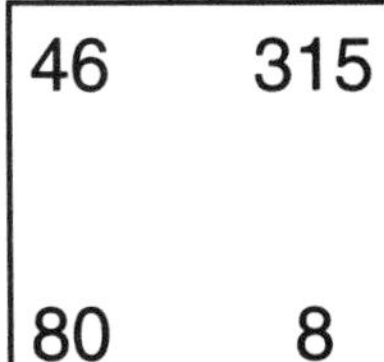

46	315
80	8

K. Estimated Product: **10,000**

511	49
21	290

L. Estimated Product: **20,000**

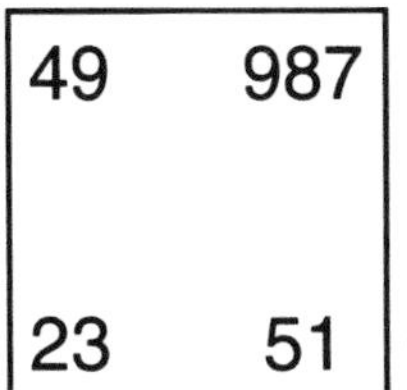

49	987
23	51

Name ____________________

A Silly Riddle

Find each product. Use the code to solve the riddle.

What has a trunk, two legs, and looks green?

S. 96 x 54

K. 38 x 77

A. 83 x 69

T. 75 x 75

A. 56 x 23

U. 49 x 48

S. 89 x 56

I. 96 x 24

S. 27 x 79

T. 37 x 65

R. 672 x 83

C. 302 x 94

I. 567 x 32

E. 489 x 86

O. 638 x 55

____ 5,727

____ 2,133 ____ 42,054 ____ 1,288 ____ 5,184 ____ 2,304 ____ 28,388 ____ 2,926

____ 2,405 ____ 35,090 ____ 2,352 ____ 55,776 ____ 18,144 ____ 4,984 ____ 5,625

Name____

Location, Location, Location

Multiply.

A. 0.72 x 3	0.16 x 4	0.32 x 5	0.09 x 8	0.7 x 6
B. 1.9 x 7	4.2 x 2	6.72 x 4	2.06 x 9	0.46 x 34
C. 3.17 x 11	6.02 x 13	0.67 x 22	5.08 x 15	6.03 x 13

Decide where the decimal point belongs in the first factor of each problem. Add the decimal point.

D. 57 x 5 = 28.5	187 x 3 = 5.61	123 x 9 = 110.7	504 x 8 = 403.2	89 x 18 = 160.2
E. 18 x 12 = 21.6	7869 x 23 = 1809.87	406 x 14 = 586.4	78 x 24 = 18.72	187 x 16 = 29.92

F. What do you notice about the number of decimal places in the factors and the products?

____

____

____

____

Name________________________________

Get the Point

Complete the table.

	Number	x 10	x 100	x 1,000	x 10,000
1.	5.1				
2.	6.43				
3.		49.8			
4.	98.6				
5.			5,270		
6.	129				
7.			41,600		
8.		1.9			
9.	0.032				
10.			75.3		
11.				0.34	
12.	81.095				

13. Describe how you would find the product of 4.357 x 1,000.

____

Name____

Fifty States

Find each product. Shade in the state that has the matching product. The states remaining were the last two states admitted into the United States of America.

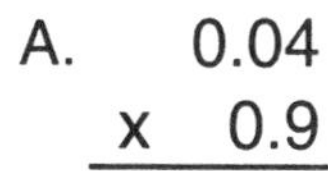

A. 0.04×0.9 | 3.8×0.05 | 0.7×0.02 | 5.3×0.08

B. 0.88×0.7 | 70×0.06 | 27.6×5.2 | 29.8×0.42 | 74.5×0.05

C. 86.3×0.86 | 0.99×0.99 | 1.42×6.3 | 5.71×3.9 | 568×0.05

Washington 0.036	**Rhode Island 22.269**	**Georgia 8.946**	**Texas 0.014**
Texas 0.9801	**South Dakota 0.19**	**Virginia 74.218**	**Hawaii 3.042**
Maryland 12.516	**Delaware 3.725**	**New York 0.424**	**California 143.52**
Alaska 5.819	**Wyoming 28.4**	**Florida 4.2**	**North Carolina 0.616**

Name ______________________________

Phone Fun

The table below shows the cost of making a telephone call from your home to various faraway cities.

City	Business Hours	Non-Business Hours
Podunk	$0.15/minute	$0.12/minute
Hoppy	$0.11/minute	$0.09/minute
Grinsville	$0.18/minute	$0.14/minute
Ringaling	$0.10/minute	$0.07/minute

Find the cost of each telephone call from your home if you called the places listed below.

1. You called Podunk during business hours for 7 minutes. ______
2. You called Hoppy during non-business hours for 12 minutes. ______
3. You called Grinsville during business hours for 15 minutes. ______
4. You called Ringaling during non-business hours for 8 minutes. ______
5. You called Podunk during non-business hours for 20 minutes. ______
6. You called Grinsville during non-business hours for 35 minutes. ______

Solve.

7. How much would you save on an 18-minute call to Grinsville by calling during non-business hours? ______
8. How much more would you spend on a 25-minute call to Hoppy if you called during business hours rather than during non-business hours? ______
9. You have $1.00 to spend. How many minutes can you spend on the telephone with your friend from Ringaling if you call during business hours? ______
10. You have $2.80 to spend. How long can you talk to your friend in Grinsville during non-business hours? ______

Name________________________________

Riddle

Turn on the Light

Who invented the light bulb?

Find the quotients. Then cross out the sections at the bottom of the page that contain the answers. The letters in the remaining squares, written in order, will spell the answer to the riddle.

A. 400 ÷ 80 = ________ 40 ÷ 10 = ________ 420 ÷ 60 = ________

B. 5,000 ÷ 500 = ________ 480 ÷ 80 = ________ 810 ÷ 90 = ________

C. 1,000 ÷ 10 = ________ 32,000 ÷ 40 = ________ 30,000 ÷ 60 = ________

D. 6,000 ÷ 300 = ________ 5,000 ÷ 100 = ________ 4,900 ÷ 70 = ________

E. 60,000 ÷ 1,000 = ________ 12,000 ÷ 400 = ________ 1,000 ÷ 40 = ________

F. 4,000 ÷ 50 = ________ 6,000 ÷ 30 = ________ 45,000 ÷ 500 = ________

T 3	F 60	H 900	K 90	O 300	J 9
Y 30	X 5	M 700	A 40	B 4	Z 200
S 600	V 70	E 1	U 500	D 8	C 7
W 80	I 1,000	Q 50	F 10	K 100	S 2,000
P 25	G 6	P 20	O 400	L 800	N 3,000

____ ____ ____ ____ ____ ____   ____ ____ ____ ____ ____ ____

Name ____

Puzzle

Puzzling Problems

Use the clues to solve the puzzle.

ACROSS

A. 6,048 ÷ 12 = ________

C. 14,848 ÷ 16 = ________

E. 31,680 ÷ 6 = ________

G. 7,056 ÷ 84 = ________

I. 0 ÷ 36 = ________

J. 98,593 ÷ 11 = ________

M. 5,240 ÷ 10 = ________

N. 948 ÷ 12 = ________

Q. 6,630 ÷ 17 = ________

R. 6,240 ÷ 20 = ________

S. 13,000 ÷ 25 = ________

DOWN

A. 11,776 ÷ 2 = ________

B. 2,070 ÷ 46 = ________

C. 8,901 ÷ 9 = ________

D. 1,780 ÷ 89 = ________

F. 31,276 ÷ 14 = ________

H. 6,435 ÷ 13 = ________

K. 68,992 ÷ 11 = ________

L. 11,376 ÷ 3 = ________

O. 9,000 ÷ 10 = ________

P. 2,211 ÷ 67 = ________

Q. 875 ÷ 25 = ________

A		B		C	D	
		E	F			
G	H					I
J		K			L	
	M				N	O
P				Q		
R				S		

Name ____________________

Matching Quotients

The quotients of two division problems in each group are the same. Use reasoning and mental math to identify the two problems. Circle your choices. Then divide to check.

A.

$6\overline{)5.4}$ $3\overline{)2.7}$

$6\overline{)10.8}$ $9\overline{)12.2}$

B.

$8\overline{)13.6}$ $4\overline{)1.36}$

$8\overline{)6.8}$ $4\overline{)6.8}$

C.

$8\overline{)28.8}$ $4\overline{)28.8}$

$4\overline{)5.76}$ $8\overline{)57.6}$

D.

$8\overline{)80.2}$ $2\overline{)40.2}$

$4\overline{)4.02}$ $8\overline{)8.04}$

E.

$4\overline{)11.4}$ $8\overline{)22.8}$

$2\overline{)22.8}$ $2\overline{)1.14}$

F.

$8\overline{)4.64}$ $4\overline{)46.4}$

$2\overline{)23.2}$ $4\overline{)9.28}$

G.

$2\overline{)12.4}$ $4\overline{)12.4}$

$4\overline{)2.48}$ $8\overline{)24.8}$

H.

$6\overline{)10.8}$ $6\overline{)2.16}$

$3\overline{)21.6}$ $3\overline{)5.4}$

Name ____________________

Unit Pricing

Write and solve each division problem to find the cost of one item.

A.

3 for $3.78

$3\overline{)3.78}$

B.

2 for $58.98

C.

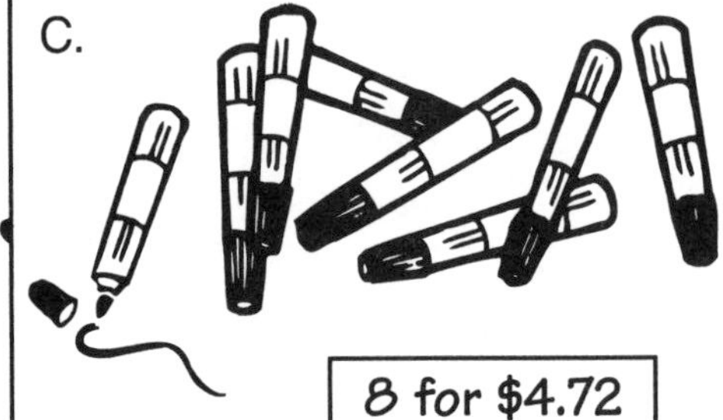

8 for $4.72

D.

6 for $27.60

E.

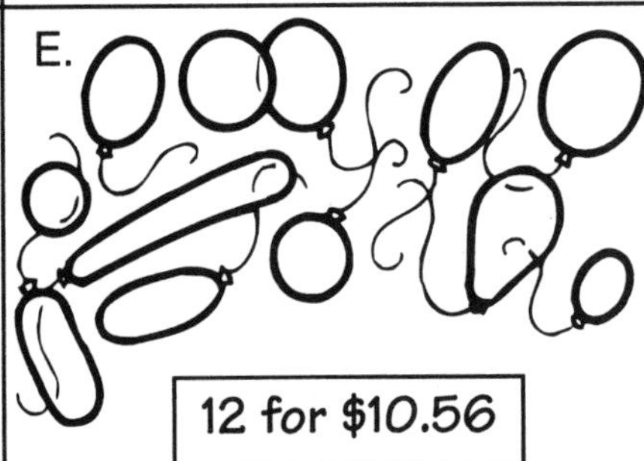

12 for $10.56

F.

10 for $1.50

G.

18 for $122.40

H.

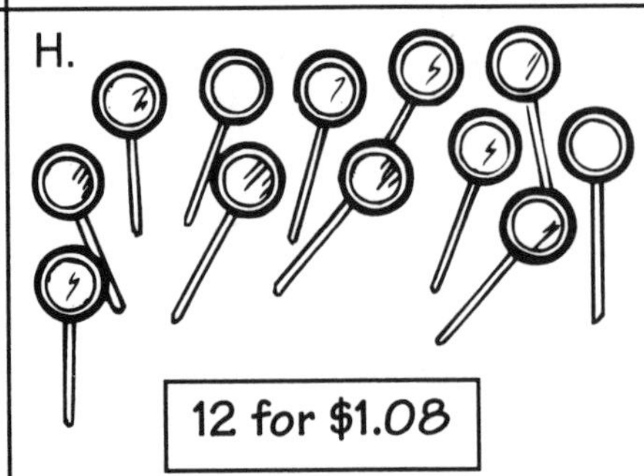

12 for $1.08

I.

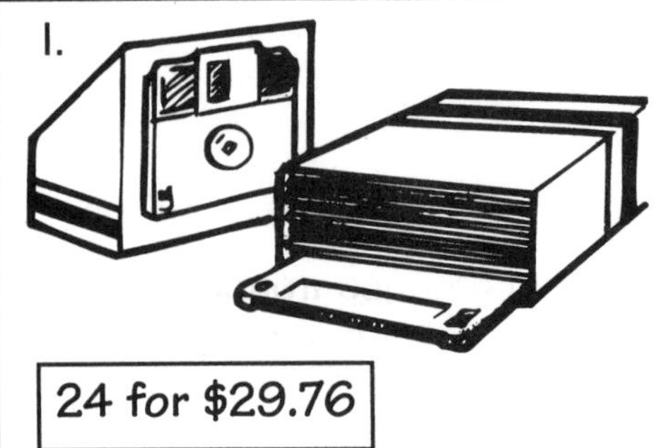

24 for $29.76

Name ____

Dancin'

Ms. Vera runs a dance troupe. She is planning this year's recital. Help Ms. Vera with her plans.

1. Ms. Vera has a 90-foot roll of ribbon left from last year's performance. How many 11-foot streamers can she make from the leftover ribbon?

   ____

2. The dance troupe recital is one hour long. Dance numbers are scheduled to last about 7 minutes. How many dance numbers can be planned for the recital?

   ____

3. At the recital, chairs are set up in rows of 12. How many rows of chairs are needed if 200 guests are expected?

   ____

4. A package of 6 buttons costs $2. How many packages of buttons can Ms. Vera purchase for $33? How many buttons will she get?

   ____

5. The dance troupe plans to spend $116 for fancy socks. Socks cost $3 for a 3-pair pack. How many 3-pair packs can Ms. Vera buy? How many pairs of socks will Ms. Vera get?

   ____

6. The dance troupe has decided to spend $185 on uniforms. New uniforms with jackets cost $33.85. Ms. Vera plans to buy 4 uniforms with jackets. Will there be enough money left over to buy any plain uniforms at the rate of $12.00 each? If so, how many uniforms could Ms. Vera buy?

   ____

   ____

Fractions and Mixed Numbers

The many activities dealing with fractions and mixed numbers in this section (pages 26–48) are a great way to help students develop and master these skills. Be sure to provide students with ample opportunities to work with manipulatives and complete several examples with your guidance. Also provide students with time for conceptual understanding before proceeding through the more independent student activity pages.

Be sure to point out how students may use their new skills in everyday life. For example, students can use their knowledge of fractions and mixed numbers when they follow recipes. Help students observe the world around them and identify their own connections to fractions and mixed numbers.

CONCEPTS

The ideas and activities presented in this section will help students explore the following concepts:

- *finding mixed numbers and improper fractions*
- *finding equivalent fractions*
- *finding greatest common factors (GCF)*
- *finding lowest term fractions*
- *finding least common denominators (LCM)*
- *adding fractions and mixed numbers*
- *subtracting fractions and mixed numbers*
- *multiplying fractions and mixed numbers*
- *dividing fractions and mixed numbers*
- *problem solving*

Understanding Fractions and Mixed Numbers

FRACTIONS IN PICTURES AND SYMBOLS

Group Activity

Have students work in pairs. One student draws a picture that represents a fraction by shading in a region or part of a set. The other student writes the fraction and labels the numerator and denominator. Students switch roles and repeat. As a variation, you may wish to have students create flashcards with picture fractions on one side and their symbolic representations (including labels for numerators and denominators) on the other.

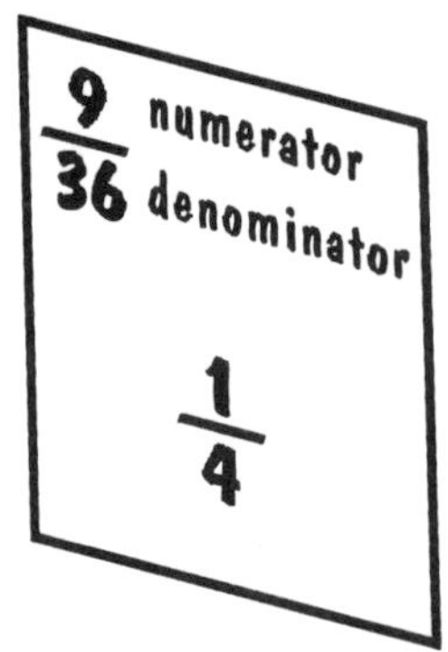

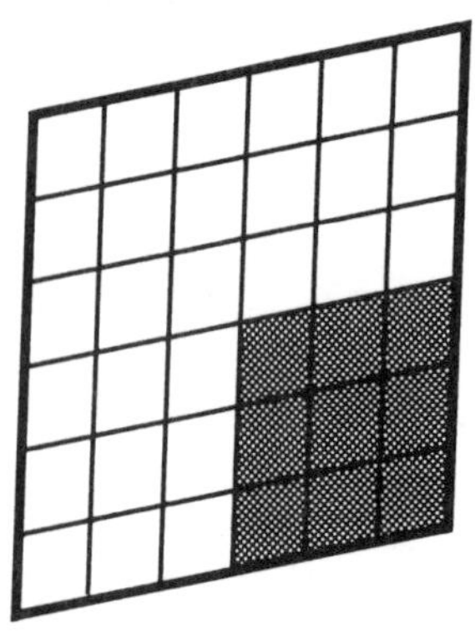

TRICKS FOR COMPARING FRACTIONS

Writing Activity

Have students write their own "tricks" for comparing fractions with the same numerators or the same denominators. Have students share their responses and test their tricks on fraction pairs such as $\frac{3}{4}$ and $\frac{3}{5}$, and $\frac{5}{12}$ and $\frac{7}{12}$. (Same numerator: smaller denominator is greater fraction. Same denominator: greater numerator is greater fraction.)

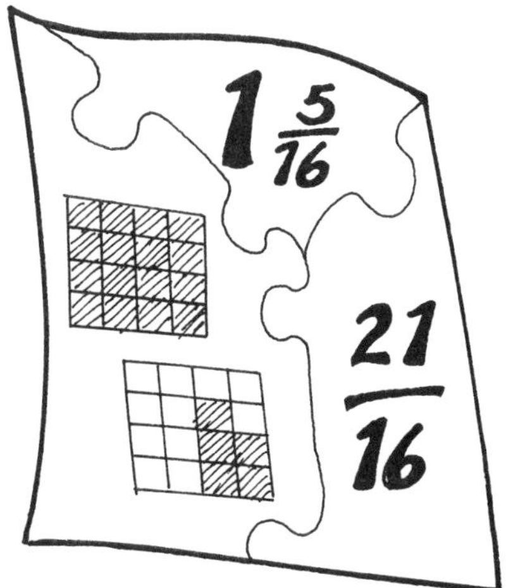

THREE-PIECE PUZZLES

Group Activity

Have students cut 8 ½" x 11" sheets of unlined paper into three-piece puzzles. Have students write one of the following on each piece: a mixed number, the equivalent improper fraction, and a model of the number. When puzzles are completed, arrange students in groups of four. Students mix their puzzle pieces on a table. Without speaking, students must work together to put the puzzles back together.

NUMBER SENSE CHALLENGE

Remind students that they find the greatest common factor (GCF) by first listing all of the factors of two (or more) numbers, and then by finding the greatest factor that appears on both lists. On the board, write a GCF. Challenge students to find two numbers whose greatest common factor is the one you wrote on the board. List students' solutions. Example: Find two numbers whose greatest common factor is 4. (Possible number pairs: 4 and 8; 8 and 12; 24 and 28)

ORDERING FRACTIONS

Game

Have small groups of students play "Between." Player A writes one fraction at the top of a sheet of paper and a greater fraction at the bottom. The sheet is passed around to the other group members who must write a fraction between the top fraction and the last fraction written. The student who wrote the first and last fraction checks the fractions for correct order. Another student in the group begins the next round and play continues.

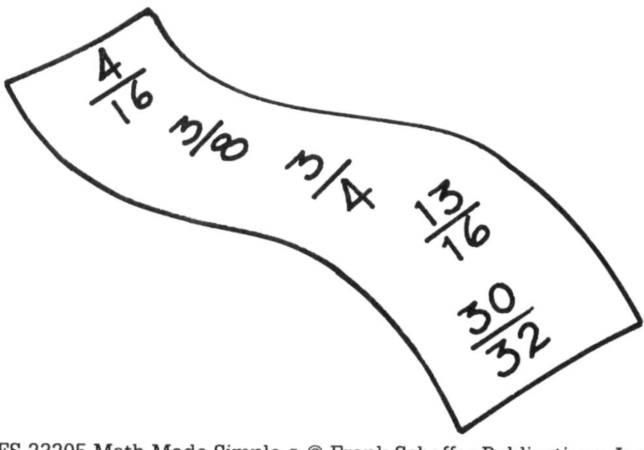

Homework

			Male	
	✓		✓	✓
		✓		✓
		✓	✓	
	✓	✓	✓	✓

School-Home Connection

Have students write descriptions of their families, including at least three sentences that involve fractions. For example, a child might write, "I have a mother, a father, and a brother. One-half of our family has brown hair. Three-fourths of us are boys. Only one-fourth of us likes lima beans." Have students illustrate their sentences and display them on a bulletin board.

Name ____________________

Mix and Match

Match each mixed number with an equivalent improper fraction.

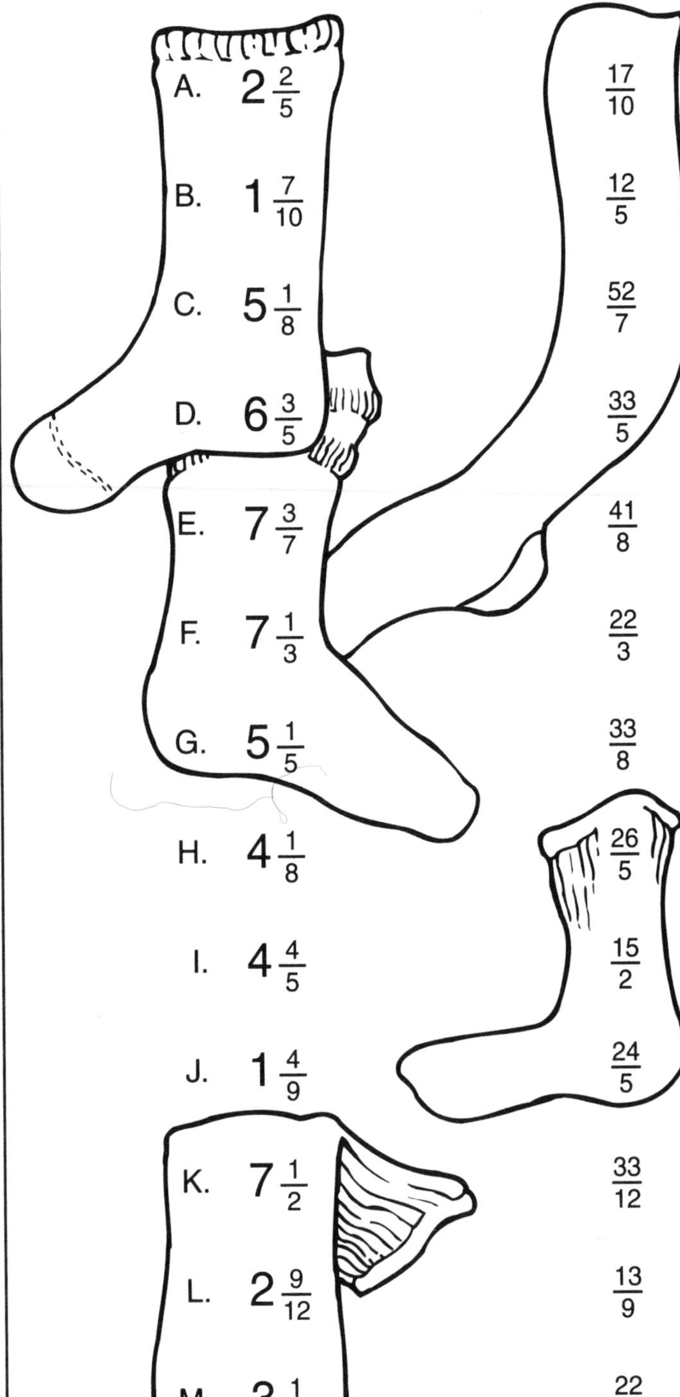

A. $2\frac{2}{5}$

B. $1\frac{7}{10}$

C. $5\frac{1}{8}$

D. $6\frac{3}{5}$

E. $7\frac{3}{7}$

F. $7\frac{1}{3}$

G. $5\frac{1}{5}$

H. $4\frac{1}{8}$

I. $4\frac{4}{5}$

J. $1\frac{4}{9}$

K. $7\frac{1}{2}$

L. $2\frac{9}{12}$

M. $3\frac{1}{7}$

$\frac{17}{10}$

$\frac{12}{5}$

$\frac{52}{7}$

$\frac{33}{5}$

$\frac{41}{8}$

$\frac{22}{3}$

$\frac{33}{8}$

$\frac{26}{5}$

$\frac{15}{2}$

$\frac{24}{5}$

$\frac{33}{12}$

$\frac{13}{9}$

$\frac{22}{7}$

N. $4\frac{5}{6}$

O. $5\frac{2}{5}$

P. $4\frac{3}{4}$

Q. $1\frac{7}{8}$

R. $6\frac{2}{3}$

S. $5\frac{4}{5}$

T. $2\frac{6}{7}$

U. $3\frac{1}{6}$

V. $3\frac{5}{8}$

W. $2\frac{3}{8}$

X. $4\frac{5}{6}$

Y. $1\frac{9}{10}$

Z. $2\frac{5}{8}$

$\frac{27}{5}$

$\frac{20}{3}$

$\frac{29}{6}$

$\frac{20}{7}$

$\frac{19}{4}$

$\frac{15}{8}$

$\frac{29}{8}$

$\frac{29}{5}$

$\frac{19}{10}$

$\frac{19}{6}$

$\frac{21}{8}$

$\frac{29}{6}$

$\frac{19}{8}$

Name________________________________

Stained Glass Window

Color each section equivalent to:

$\frac{1}{2}$ — green $\frac{1}{3}$ — blue $\frac{1}{4}$ — yellow $\frac{2}{5}$ — red

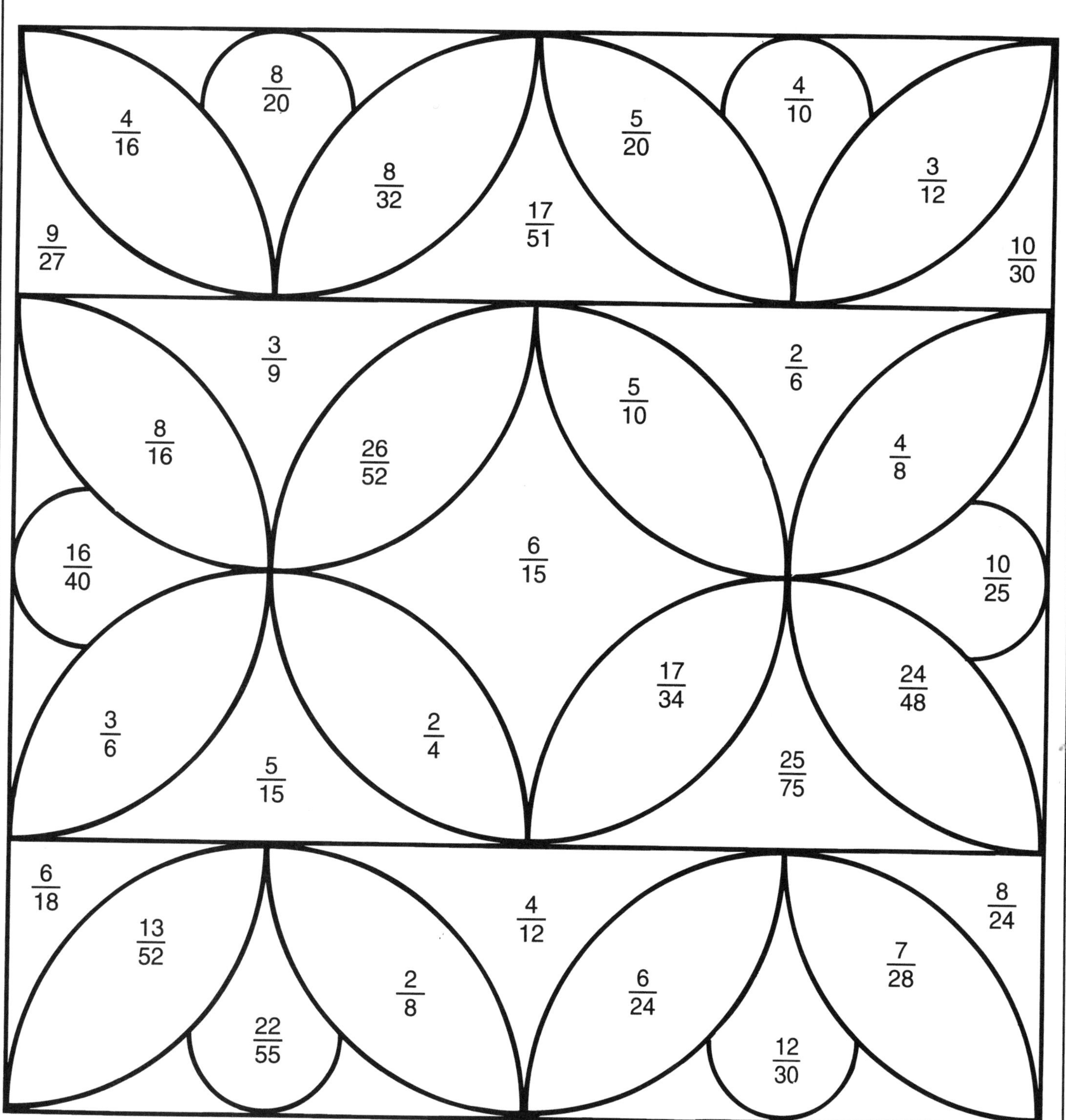

Name ______________________________

Riddle

The Highest Peak

Find the greatest common factor (GCF) for each pair of numbers. Then cross out one square at the bottom of the page that contains the answer. The letters to the remaining squares, written in order, will spell the answer to the following question:

What is the highest mountain peak in the world?

A. 12 and 30 GCF = ______

B. 8 and 10 GCF = ______

C. 6 and 12 GCF = ______

D. 21 and 35 GCF = ______

E. 12 and 18 GCF = ______

F. 15 and 40 GCF = ______

G. 16 and 24 GCF = ______

H. 21 and 45 GCF = ______

I. 18 and 30 GCF = ______

J. 22 and 52 GCF = ______

16 and 20 GCF = ______

7 and 9 GCF = ______

9 and 12 GCF = ______

10 and 16 GCF = ______

14 and 21 GCF = ______

36 and 48 GCF = ______

18 and 36 GCF = ______

24 and 42 GCF = ______

45 and 54 GCF = ______

16 and 64 GCF = ______

M 0	A 4	C 6	O 30	J 5	H 2	U 11	L 12
P 6	N 15	Q 3	B 7	T 10	H 6	Y 8	E 13
Z 18	U 7	V 22	G 3	X 1	E 20	R 14	K 6
F 2	E 17	W 6	S 21	C 9	J 2	D 16	T 25

___ ___ ___ ___ ___   ___ ___ ___ ___ ___ ___ ___

Name ____________________

Secret Message

A Shaded Message

Rewrite each fraction below in lowest terms. If the fraction is already in lowest terms, simply shade in the section. The shaded area will reveal what you might have used to solve the problems on this page.

A.	$\frac{6}{8}$ =	$\frac{3}{15}$ =	$\frac{15}{21}$ =	$\frac{9}{36}$ =	$\frac{3}{24}$ =
B.	$\frac{15}{18}$ =	$\frac{18}{24}$ =	$\frac{3}{8}$ =	$\frac{8}{20}$ =	$\frac{9}{18}$ =
C.	$\frac{4}{100}$ =	$\frac{9}{12}$ =	$\frac{10}{24}$ =	$\frac{12}{15}$ =	$\frac{16}{18}$ =
D.	$\frac{6}{13}$ =	$\frac{2}{5}$ =	$\frac{3}{4}$ =	$\frac{15}{22}$ =	$\frac{8}{9}$ =
E.	$\frac{12}{23}$ =	$\frac{7}{8}$ =	$\frac{4}{15}$ =	$\frac{6}{25}$ =	$\frac{1}{5}$ =
F.	$\frac{18}{45}$ =	$\frac{36}{40}$ =	$\frac{6}{60}$ =	$\frac{35}{42}$ =	$\frac{6}{16}$ =
G.	$\frac{12}{30}$ =	$\frac{18}{27}$ =	$\frac{7}{24}$ =	$\frac{25}{30}$ =	$\frac{34}{50}$ =
H.	$\frac{60}{70}$ =	$\frac{12}{32}$ =	$\frac{13}{52}$ =	$\frac{28}{56}$ =	$\frac{16}{48}$ =
I.	$\frac{9}{30}$ =	$\frac{50}{75}$ =	$\frac{34}{51}$ =	$\frac{24}{96}$ =	$\frac{63}{81}$ =

Name ______________________________

The Factor and Multiple Trick

Find the greatest common factor (GCF) and the least common multiple (LCM) for each pair of numbers below. Next, find the product of the GCF and LCM and the product of the two numbers. What do you notice?

Remember:

To find the GCF, list the factors of each number. Then find the greatest factor on both lists.

To find the LCM, list multiples of each number. Find the first multiple on both lists.

A. **4, 6**	B. **6, 9**	C. **5, 15**
GCF 2 LCM 12 a. GCF x LCM = 24 b. 4 x 6 = 24	GCF ___ LCM ___ a. GCF x LCM = ___ b. 6 x 9 = ___	GCF ___ LCM ___ a. GCF x LCM = ___ b. 5 x 15 = ___
D. **10, 12** GCF ___ LCM ___ a. GCF x LCM = ___ b. 10 x 12 = ___	E. **9, 12** GCF ___ LCM ___ a. GCF x LCM = ___ b. 9 x 12 = ___	F. **12, 18** GCF ___ LCM ___ a. GCF x LCM = ___ b. 12 x 18 = ___
G. **6, 8** GCF ___ LCM ___ a. GCF x LCM = ___ b. 6 x 8 = ___	H. **8, 20** GCF ___ LCM ___ a. GCF x LCM = ___ b. 8 x 20 = ___	I. **9, 24** GCF ___ LCM ___ a. GCF x LCM = ___ b. 9 x 24 = ___

What did you notice about A and B? ______________________________

Name________________________________

Fraction Paths

Draw arrows to show the order from the smallest fraction to the largest. Circle the largest fraction in each group.

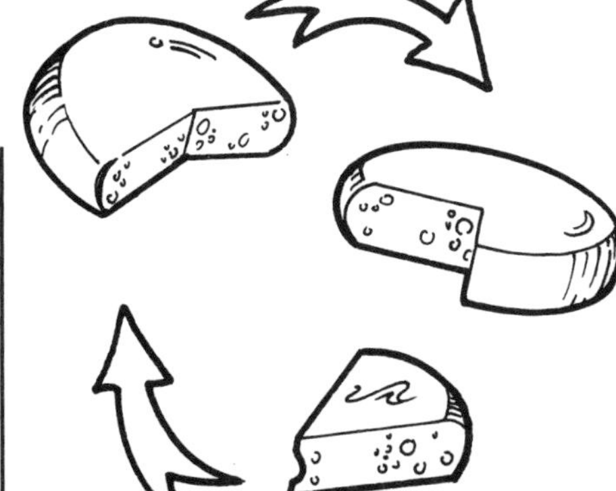

A. $\frac{3}{8}$ $\frac{1}{2}$ $\frac{1}{4}$

B. $\frac{3}{4}$ $\frac{5}{8}$ $\frac{1}{3}$

C. $\frac{1}{3}$ $\frac{7}{12}$ $\frac{3}{10}$

D. $\frac{1}{2}$ $\frac{5}{8}$ $\frac{2}{5}$

E. $\frac{2}{3}$ $\frac{3}{5}$ $\frac{3}{8}$

F. $\frac{7}{12}$ $\frac{3}{4}$ $\frac{4}{5}$

G. $\frac{5}{6}$ $\frac{2}{3}$ $\frac{7}{8}$

H. $\frac{8}{9}$ $\frac{5}{8}$ $\frac{7}{9}$

I. $\frac{3}{5}$ $\frac{2}{7}$ $\frac{4}{9}$

J. $\frac{2}{3}$ $\frac{3}{4}$ $\frac{1}{2}$ $\frac{4}{5}$

K. $\frac{7}{10}$ $\frac{8}{10}$ $\frac{3}{4}$ $\frac{2}{3}$

L. $\frac{3}{10}$ $\frac{3}{8}$ $\frac{2}{5}$ $\frac{1}{4}$

M. $\frac{3}{10}$ $\frac{5}{12}$ $\frac{3}{4}$ $\frac{1}{2}$

N. $\frac{19}{20}$ $\frac{17}{20}$ $\frac{9}{10}$ $\frac{2}{3}$

Adding, Subtracting, Multiplying, and Dividing Fractions and Mixed Numbers

FRACTION SUMS AND DIFFERENCES

Group Activity

Have students work in groups of four. Student A writes a fraction whose numerator is greater than 1. Student B writes a fraction with a lesser value using the same denominator. Student C finds the sum of the two fractions, and Student D finds their difference. Students repeat the process so that every student has a chance to do each part of the activity.

FRACTION FUN

Manipulative Activities

Fraction Model Sums and Differences

Provide students with fraction pieces. Have them use the models to show and solve addition problems. You may wish to suggest that students use the fraction pieces to help them find their answers in lowest terms. Use problems such as $\frac{1}{4} + \frac{1}{4}$ ($\frac{2}{4}$ or $\frac{1}{2}$); $\frac{1}{3} + \frac{1}{3}$ ($\frac{2}{3}$); $\frac{1}{8} + \frac{5}{8}$ ($\frac{6}{8}$ or $\frac{3}{4}$).

Subtracting With Fraction Pieces

Provide groups of students with fraction wholes and fraction pieces. Have them work together to find differences of (a) two mixed numbers with like denominators, such as $3\frac{4}{5} - 1\frac{2}{5}$ ($2\frac{2}{5}$) or $5\frac{1}{3} - 1\frac{2}{3}$ ($3\frac{2}{3}$); (b) two mixed numbers with unlike denominators, such as $4\frac{3}{4} - 1\frac{1}{2}$ ($3\frac{1}{4}$) or $5\frac{1}{8} - 2\frac{1}{2}$ ($2\frac{5}{8}$); and (c) a whole number and a mixed number, such as $4 - 1\frac{5}{6}$ ($2\frac{1}{6}$). Have students discuss how they used the pieces to help them regroup.

ESTIMATING FRACTIONAL SUMS AND DIFFERENCES

Writing Activity

List the following mixed numbers on the board:

$3\frac{1}{3}$ $4\frac{1}{4}$ $5\frac{3}{8}$ $2\frac{4}{9}$

$3\frac{4}{7}$ $4\frac{11}{12}$ $5\frac{1}{8}$

Have pairs of students challenge each other to find a sum or a difference closest to a given amount. For example, one student may challenge another to find two numbers whose difference is closest to 2 ($5\frac{3}{8}$ and $3\frac{1}{3}$).

Stock Time

Finance Connection

Have each student bring to class the financial section of a local newspaper. Have each student pick five stocks. Students are to record the high and low for each stock every day for a 5-day period. Then students can estimate the difference between the highs and lows for each day. Ask students if they see any trends in the movements of the stocks (i.e., are they increasing or decreasing in value?).

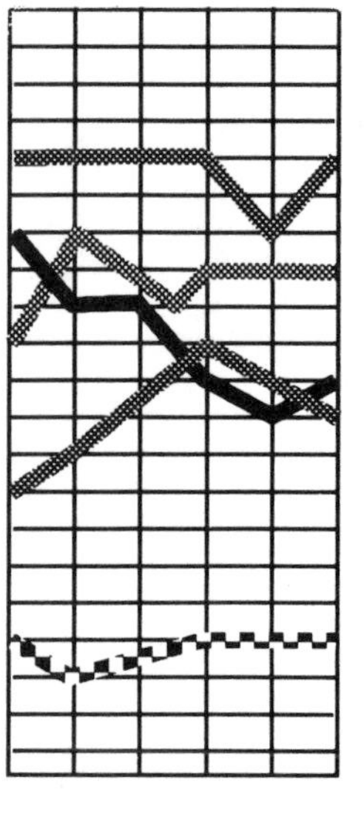

Class Activity

Fraction Riddles

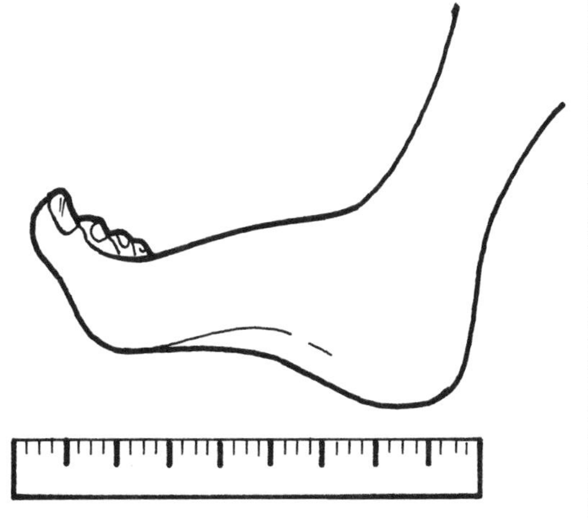

Have students solve riddles such as the following:

a. When can a foot be a $\frac{1}{2}$ foot? (When a person's foot is 6 inches long)

b. If a quarter of a quart of milk costs a quarter, how much will a quart cost? ($1.00)

c. How can a person who gained weight be a fraction of his or her former weight? (His or her weight can be shown as an improper fraction.)

Challenge students to make up their own silly fraction riddles and share them with the class.

ESTIMATING PRODUCTS

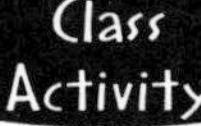

Write a problem such as $\frac{3}{4}$ x $\frac{1}{3}$ or $\frac{3}{4}$ of $\frac{1}{3}$ on an overhead. Have students discuss what they can determine about the size of the answer without solving the problem. To help them, ask leading questions such as *Will the product be greater than 1? greater than $\frac{3}{4}$? greater than $\frac{1}{3}$? less than $\frac{3}{4}$? less than $\frac{1}{3}$? less than 0? Explain.* (It will be less than $\frac{3}{4}$ or $\frac{1}{3}$, since it is part of a part.) Repeat the process for a variety of other factor pairs such as $1\frac{1}{2}$ x $\frac{1}{2}$ or 3 x $\frac{3}{4}$. Finally, help students form some generalizations about products when fractions are one or more of the factors, and have students write about it in their journals.

FRACTION NUMBER PATTERN SEQUENCE

Class Activity

Have students state the rule and find the next two numbers in sequences such as the following:

a. $1\frac{2}{3}$, $2\frac{1}{3}$, 3 (add $\frac{2}{3}$; $3\frac{2}{3}$, $4\frac{1}{3}$)

b. $2\frac{4}{5}$, $3\frac{2}{5}$, 4 (add $\frac{3}{5}$; $4\frac{3}{5}$; $5\frac{1}{5}$)

c. $1\frac{5}{8}$, 3, $4\frac{3}{8}$ (add $1\frac{3}{8}$; $5\frac{3}{4}$, $7\frac{1}{8}$)

d. $3\frac{7}{12}$, $3\frac{1}{12}$, $2\frac{7}{12}$ (subtract $\frac{6}{12}$; $2\frac{1}{12}$, $1\frac{7}{12}$)

KEEP 'EM ROLLING

Game

Have students use self-adhesive dots to cover each side of two number cubes with the following mixed numbers:

Cube A: $1\frac{2}{3}$; $1\frac{2}{5}$; $3\frac{1}{5}$; $1\frac{3}{4}$; $2\frac{1}{2}$; $1\frac{7}{8}$.

Cube B: $1\frac{1}{4}$; $3\frac{1}{3}$; $5\frac{1}{2}$; $2\frac{4}{5}$; $3\frac{1}{2}$; $2\frac{3}{8}$.

Students play in pairs or small groups. One student rolls the number cubes and then gives the estimated sum or estimated difference of the two numbers rolled. The other students determine whether the estimate is reasonable by performing the operation and finding the actual answer. If the estimate is reasonable, the player scores a point. The first player to reach three points wins the round.

PRODUCTS AND QUOTIENTS WITH FRACTION PIECES

Manipulative Activity

Have students work in pairs and use fraction pieces to solve the following problems:

a. $\frac{1}{2} \times 1\frac{1}{2}$ ($\frac{3}{4}$)   b. $\frac{1}{3} \times \frac{3}{4}$ ($\frac{1}{4}$)   c. $\frac{1}{4} \times 3$ ($\frac{3}{4}$)

d. $\frac{2}{3} \times 4\frac{1}{2}$ (3)   e. $\frac{3}{4} \times \frac{1}{2}$ ($\frac{3}{8}$)   f. $\frac{1}{4} \times 6$ ($1\frac{1}{2}$)

g. $3 \div \frac{1}{3}$ (9)   h. $1 \div \frac{1}{4}$ (4)   i. $2 \div \frac{1}{2}$ (4)

Have students trace and shade their fraction pieces to record their work in their journals.

BALANCE MIXED NUMBERS

Class Activity

Tell students to imagine that they have the following small weights:

$\frac{1}{8}$ pound $\frac{1}{4}$ pound $\frac{3}{8}$ pound $\frac{1}{2}$ pound $\frac{3}{4}$ pound

Challenge students to find combinations that would make a total of $1\frac{1}{2}$ pounds. Construct a list of all correct responses. Then have students determine a new target number and play again.

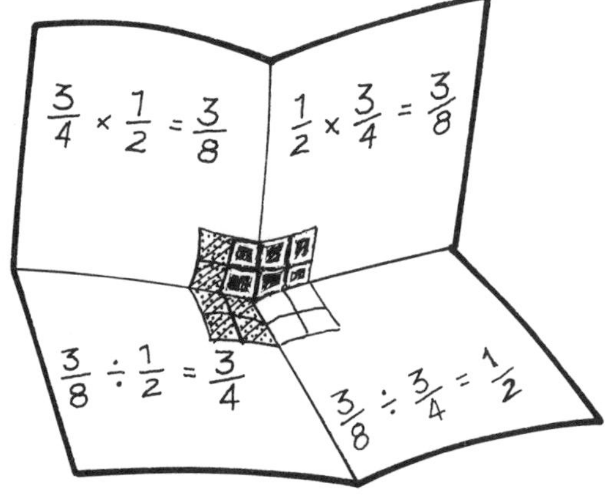

FRACTION FAMILIES

Class Activity

Supply each student with a sheet of plain paper and colored pencils. Students fold their papers into 4 sections. They write a multiplication equation using one or more fractions (such as $\frac{3}{4} \times \frac{1}{2} = \frac{3}{8}$) in one section. They write the related multiplication equation in another section ($\frac{1}{2} \times \frac{3}{4} = \frac{3}{8}$). In the last two sections, students write the related division equations ($\frac{3}{8} \div \frac{1}{2} = \frac{3}{4}$ and $\frac{3}{8} \div \frac{3}{4} = \frac{1}{2}$). Students may sketch illustrations for their fraction families in the foldlines of their pages. Put finished papers on a bulletin board for classmates to examine.

Finance Connection

Paper Folding

Have each student fold a sheet of yellow or white construction paper in half four times. After each fold, have students predict, then check, how many sections they have. Once they have completed the folding and have 16 sections, students should color part of the sections. Then each student can write an equation telling what part of the sheet is colored in and how many sections it has. (Example: $\frac{1}{2} \times 16 = 8$) You can also have students predict how many sections there would be if their papers were folded 10 times (20 sections), 20 times (40 sections), etc.

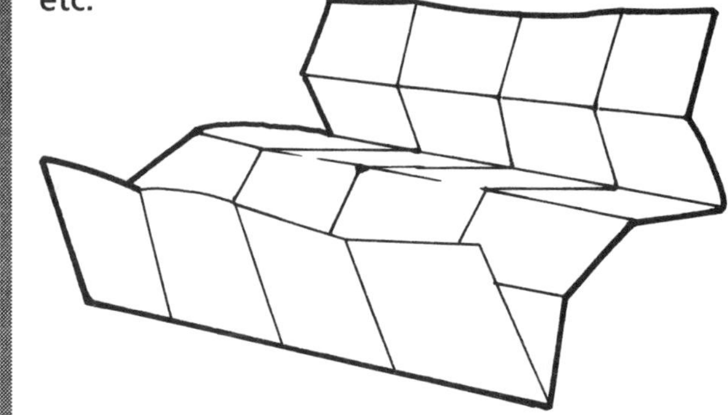

FRACTION TERMS

Writing Activity

Write the following terms on an overhead: *fraction, like, unlike, numerator, denominator, equivalent fraction, fraction pieces.* Have students work in pairs to write a step-by-step approach in their journals to adding ⅔ and ¾ using fraction pieces. Suggest to students that they should use the words on the overhead as they write their directions. They can also highlight or underline these words when they are finished writing.

fraction 2/3

3/4 numerator

like denominator

8/12

unlike

9/12

equivalent fraction

fraction pieces

Homework

School-Home Connection

Pizza Pie Fun

Have students use a pizza (or another food item that could easily be cut into pieces) for this activity. Family members can take turns modeling fractions using pieces of the pizza and showing equivalent fractions. When completed, students and family members can eat the pieces.

Follow This Recipe!

Encourage students to follow a recipe with family members. They can help measure the ingredients and estimate the total number of cups, quarts, or pounds the completed recipe will yield.

Money Fun

Have students and their families find fractional parts of numbers using collections of pennies. Students should begin with 6 pennies. They can find ⅓ of the set (2¢), ½ of the set (3¢), and ⅙ of the set (1¢). The process may be repeated using 12 pennies, 18 pennies, and 24 pennies. Students may record their work with equations such as ⅓ of 6 = 2; ½ of 6 = 3; ⅙ of 6 = 1, and so on.

Name________________________________

Matching Models

Match each sum with the model that shows the lowest term answer. Use your answers to break the code and answer the following riddle:

What do you call a driver who has had no accidents?

1. $\frac{1}{2} + \frac{1}{3} =$ ______
2. $\frac{1}{12} + \frac{1}{4} =$ ______
3. $\frac{1}{2} + \frac{1}{4} =$ ______
4. $\frac{2}{8} + \frac{1}{4} =$ ______
5. $\frac{1}{5} + \frac{1}{10} =$ ______
6. $\frac{1}{4} + \frac{1}{8} =$ ______
7. $\frac{1}{5} + \frac{7}{10} =$ ______
8. $\frac{1}{6} + \frac{1}{3} =$ ______
9. $\frac{3}{4} + \frac{1}{8} =$ ______
10. $\frac{1}{4} + \frac{5}{8} =$ ______
11. $\frac{1}{12} + \frac{1}{6} =$ ______
12. $\frac{3}{12} + \frac{1}{2} =$ ______
13. $\frac{1}{2} + \frac{1}{6} =$ ______
14. $\frac{1}{2} + \frac{1}{8} =$ ______
15. $\frac{2}{5} + \frac{1}{10} =$ ______
16. $\frac{7}{12} + \frac{1}{6} =$ ______

W
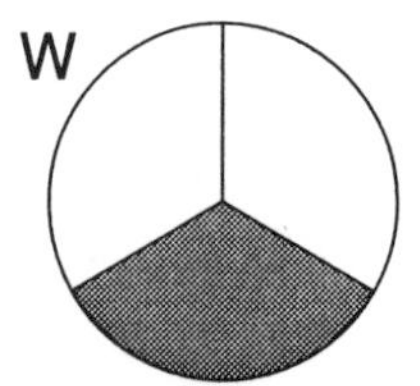

D
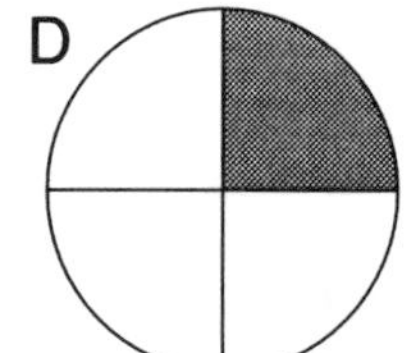

R
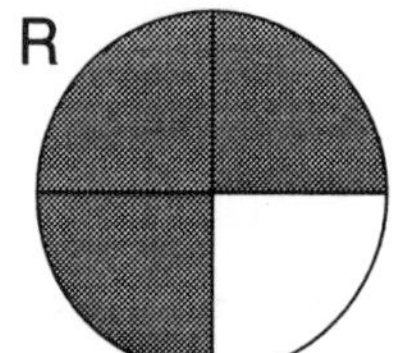

L
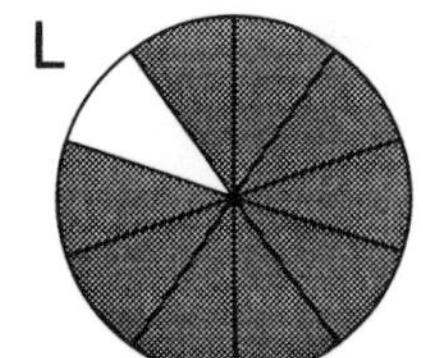

E
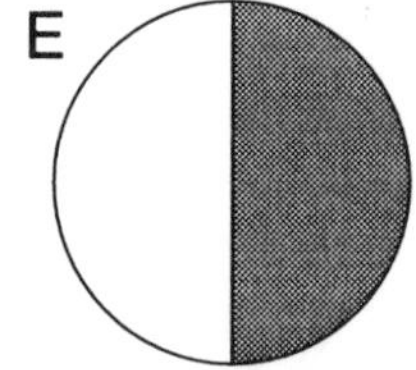

V
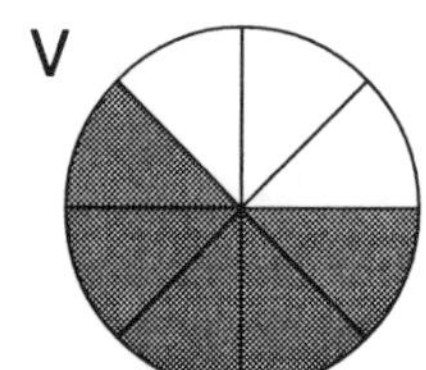

S
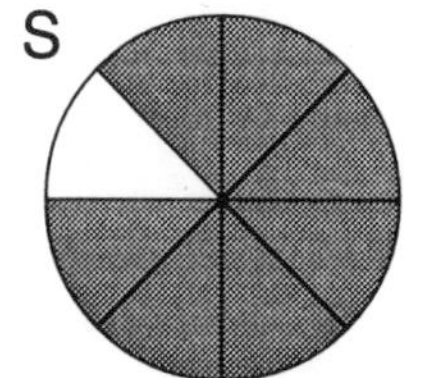

C
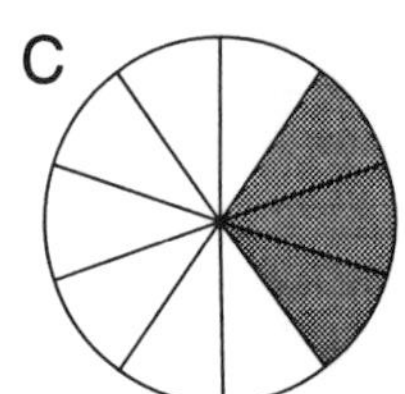

I
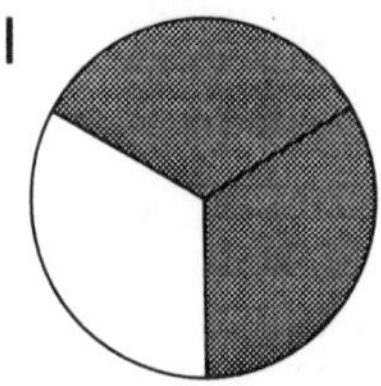

K
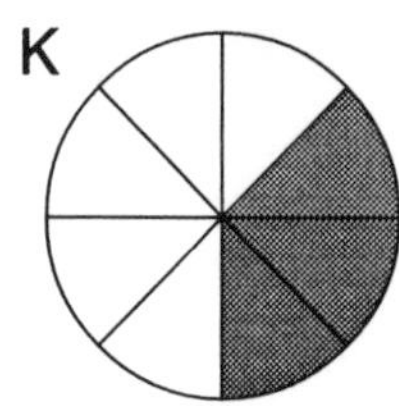

A
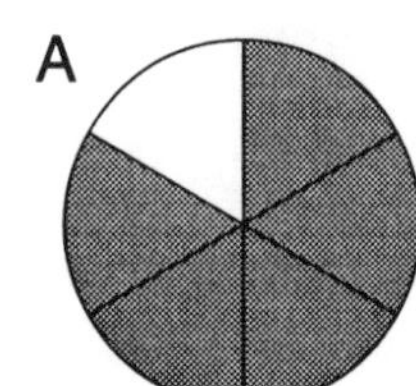

___ 1   ___ 2   ___ 3   ___ 4   ___ 5   ___ 6   ___ 7   ___ 8   ___ 9   ___ 10

___ 11   ___ 12   ___ 13   ___ 14   ___ 15   ___ 16

Name ______________________________

Word Values

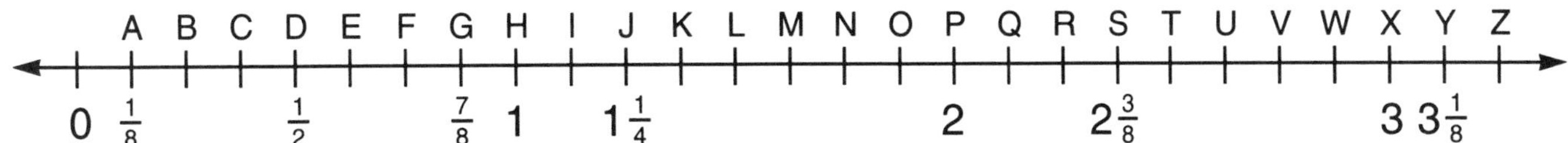

1. Find the value of each letter.

A. ______ E. ______ I. ______ O. ______ U. ______ L. ______

R. ______ T. ______ W. ______ M. ______ K. ______ N. ______

Find the total value of each word. Write an addition sentence to help. Write your answer in lowest terms.

2. AM	3. IN	4. NO
5. MY	6. HE	7. IS
8. YES	9. ADD	10. MATH

11. Find the total value of your name.	12. Find the total value of any 5-letter word.

Name____

Pop!

Add. Color the balloon with the sum that matches.

A. $1\frac{1}{5} + 3\frac{1}{2}$ $\qquad$ $2\frac{1}{8} + 3\frac{1}{4}$

B. $3\frac{1}{8} + 2\frac{3}{4}$ $\qquad$ $4\frac{1}{3} + 4\frac{1}{6}$

C. $5\frac{2}{3} + 2\frac{1}{5}$ $\qquad$ $7\frac{1}{2} + 1\frac{3}{4}$

D. $1\frac{7}{8} + 3\frac{5}{6}$ $\qquad$ $4\frac{2}{5} + 3\frac{7}{10}$

E. $2\frac{2}{5} + 4\frac{5}{6}$ $\qquad$ $2\frac{1}{4} + 3\frac{9}{10}$ $\qquad$ $6\frac{1}{2} + 3\frac{6}{7}$ $\qquad$ $4\frac{2}{3} + 5\frac{1}{5}$

F. $2\frac{4}{5} + 3\frac{1}{20}$ $\qquad$ $2\frac{5}{6} + 1\frac{3}{4}$ $\qquad$ $3\frac{5}{6} + \frac{1}{3}$ $\qquad$ $6\frac{7}{10} + \frac{4}{5}$

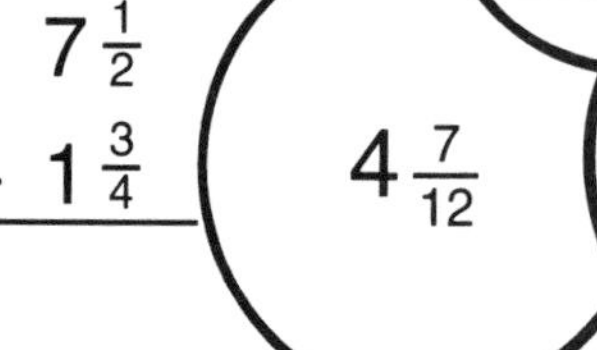

G. What is the sum of the remaining balloons? Write a number sentence and solve.

Name ______________________________

Famous Inventions

Subtract. Use your answers to break the code and find out why Alexander Graham Bell is famous.

P. $6\frac{7}{8} - 1\frac{1}{2}$	V. $2\frac{1}{5} - 1\frac{1}{2}$	E. $4\frac{4}{7} - 1\frac{2}{5}$	T. $9\frac{7}{8} - \frac{1}{3}$	H. $4\frac{3}{4} - 1\frac{1}{2}$
E. $8\frac{3}{8} - 5\frac{1}{16}$	I. $6\frac{4}{5} - 4\frac{3}{10}$	E. $8\frac{1}{2} - 3\frac{1}{5}$	N. $2\frac{9}{10} - 1\frac{4}{5}$	D. $5\frac{1}{8} - 2$
N. $2\frac{1}{3} - \frac{1}{5}$	T. $9\frac{2}{3} - 3\frac{1}{5}$	O. $1\frac{3}{8} - \frac{1}{12}$	H. $8\frac{1}{3} - 3\frac{1}{2}$	T. $7\frac{1}{8} - 1\frac{1}{4}$
E. $5\frac{2}{5} - 3\frac{7}{10}$	H. $7 - 1\frac{1}{2}$	E. $2\frac{1}{12} - 1\frac{5}{6}$	L. $6\frac{1}{2} - 5\frac{3}{4}$	E. $9\frac{3}{10} - 1\frac{3}{5}$

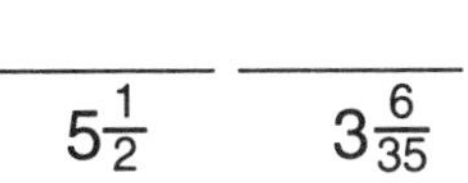

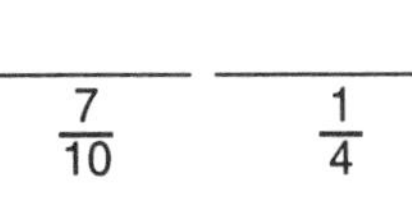

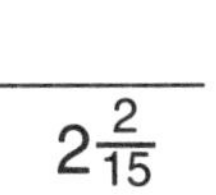

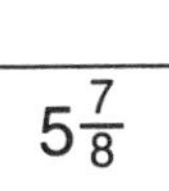

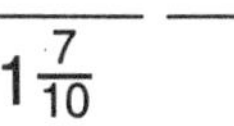

___ $5\frac{1}{2}$ ___ $3\frac{6}{35}$ ___ $2\frac{1}{2}$ N ___ $\frac{7}{10}$ ___ $\frac{1}{4}$ ___ $2\frac{2}{15}$ ___ $5\frac{7}{8}$ ___ $1\frac{7}{10}$ ___ $3\frac{1}{8}$

___ $6\frac{7}{15}$ ___ $4\frac{5}{6}$ ___ $3\frac{5}{16}$

___ $9\frac{13}{24}$ ___ $5\frac{3}{10}$ ___ $\frac{3}{4}$ E ___ $5\frac{3}{8}$ ___ $3\frac{1}{4}$ ___ $1\frac{7}{24}$ ___ $1\frac{1}{10}$ ___ $7\frac{7}{10}$.

Name____

Magic Squares

Fraction Square Magic

Complete each square so that the sums of the numbers across and down match the magic number square.

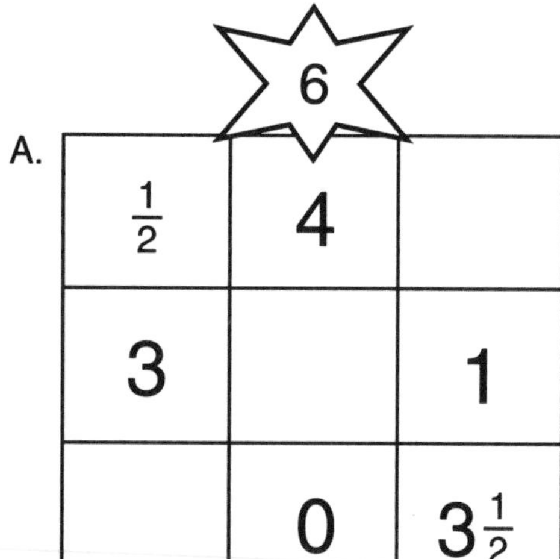

A. Magic number: 6

$\frac{1}{2}$	4	
3		1
	0	$3\frac{1}{2}$

B. Magic number: 3

	$1\frac{2}{5}$	$1\frac{1}{5}$
$1\frac{4}{5}$		
	$\frac{3}{5}$	$1\frac{3}{5}$

C. Magic number: $2\frac{1}{2}$

$\frac{1}{2}$		1
	$\frac{3}{4}$	$\frac{1}{4}$
$\frac{1}{2}$		

D. Magic number: $3\frac{3}{4}$

	$\frac{1}{4}$	$1\frac{1}{2}$
$\frac{3}{4}$		$1\frac{3}{4}$
	$2\frac{1}{2}$	

E. Magic number: $4\frac{1}{4}$

	$1\frac{1}{2}$	
$\frac{5}{8}$		$1\frac{1}{4}$
	$\frac{3}{8}$	$2\frac{1}{4}$

F. Magic number: $1\frac{7}{8}$

$\frac{1}{2}$		1
	$\frac{5}{8}$	
$\frac{1}{4}$		$\frac{3}{4}$

Name ______________________________

Run for Fun and Fitness

Anna and Robyn run every day. They record their distances in a table.

Running Log (in miles)

Day	Monday	Tuesday	Wednesday	Thursday	Friday
Anna	3 ½	4 ¾	3 ½	5	5 ¾
Robyn	3 ⅞	4	4 ¼	4 ⅞	5 ⅝

Solve. Write addition or subtraction equations to help you.

1. How far did Anna run on Monday and Tuesday? ___________
2. How far did Robyn run on Wednesday and Thursday? ___________
3. On which day was Robyn and Anna's combined distance least? greatest?

   ____

4. Who ran farther on Monday? By how many miles?

   ____

5. Who ran farther on Thursday? By how many miles?

   ____

6. Estimate the total number of miles run by each runner for the five-day period.

   ____

7. On which day did Anna and Robyn run a total of about 10 miles?

   ____

8. On which day did Robyn run more than ½ mile farther than Anna?

   ____

Name____

Fishbowl Products

Solve.

A. $\frac{1}{2} \times \frac{1}{3} =$ ______

B. $\frac{3}{4} \times \frac{1}{2} =$ ______

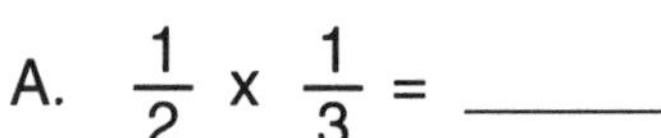

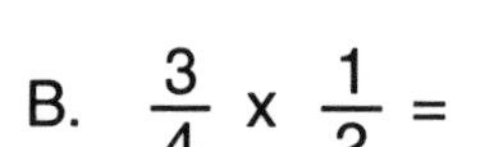

C. $\frac{2}{3} \times \frac{1}{4} =$ ______

D. $\frac{2}{5} \times \frac{1}{2} =$ ______

E. $\frac{5}{8} \times \frac{1}{3} =$ ______

F. $\frac{3}{5} \times \frac{2}{3} =$ ______

G. $\frac{4}{5} \times \frac{3}{4} =$ ______

H. $\frac{2}{3} \times \frac{3}{4} =$ ______

I. $\frac{2}{5} \times \frac{10}{11} =$ ______

J. $\frac{3}{7} \times \frac{7}{9} =$ ______

K. $\frac{1}{2} \times \frac{8}{13} =$ ______

L. $\frac{3}{4} \times \frac{8}{15} =$ ______

M. $\frac{7}{10} \times \frac{2}{3} =$ ______

N. $\frac{5}{6} \times \frac{10}{11} =$ ______

O. $\frac{1}{2} \times \frac{9}{10} =$ ______

Name________________________________

Riddle

Fraction Product Riddle

Multiply. Use your answers to break the code and solve the following riddle:

Why did Sam take a hammer to bed?

B. $\frac{1}{8} \times \frac{1}{7} =$ ______

H. $\frac{1}{3} \times \frac{4}{7} =$ ______

W. $2 \times \frac{3}{5} =$ ______

T. $\frac{5}{9} \times \frac{2}{3} =$ ______

H. $\frac{2}{7} \times \frac{2}{7} =$ ______

T. $\frac{5}{6} \times 4 =$ ______

H. $\frac{1}{3} \times 6 =$ ______

E. $\frac{8}{9} \times \frac{1}{3} =$ ______

E. $\frac{2}{5} \times \frac{4}{7} =$ ______

A. $\frac{1}{4} \times \frac{2}{3} =$ ______

O. $\frac{2}{5} \times \frac{1}{4} =$ ______

I. $\frac{3}{8} \times \frac{1}{2} =$ ______

H. $\frac{1}{6} \times 8 =$ ______

A. $8 \times \frac{3}{5} =$ ______

C. $\frac{4}{5} \times \frac{1}{4} =$ ______

N. $\frac{2}{7} \times \frac{7}{8} =$ ______

T. $\frac{4}{5} \times \frac{1}{6} =$ ______

E. $\frac{1}{10} \times 5 =$ ______

Y. $\frac{5}{12} \times \frac{1}{3} =$ ______

A. $\frac{2}{3} \times \frac{5}{8} =$ ______

T. $7 \times \frac{1}{3} =$ ______

U. $\frac{2}{3} \times \frac{2}{5} =$ ______

E. $9 \times \frac{2}{3} =$ ______

S. $\frac{5}{8} \times \frac{4}{9} =$ ______

___ ___ ___ ___ ___ ___ E   ___ ___

$\frac{1}{56}$ $\frac{8}{27}$ $\frac{1}{5}$ $\frac{1}{6}$ $\frac{4}{15}$ $\frac{5}{18}$ $\frac{4}{21}$ $\frac{8}{35}$

___ ___ ___ ___ ___ D   ___ ___

$1\frac{1}{5}$ $4\frac{4}{5}$ $\frac{1}{4}$ $\frac{10}{27}$ $\frac{1}{2}$ $3\frac{1}{3}$ $\frac{1}{10}$

___ ___ ___   ___ ___ ___   ___ ___ ___

$\frac{4}{49}$ $\frac{3}{16}$ $\frac{2}{15}$ $2\frac{1}{3}$ 2 6 $1\frac{1}{3}$ $\frac{5}{12}$ $\frac{5}{36}$

Name______________________________

Puzzle

Tic-Tac Products

Use the tic-tac-toe board to find the factors and write each multiplication equation. Then write the products in lowest terms.

$3\frac{1}{3}$	$\frac{4}{5}$	$2\frac{1}{2}$
$5\frac{1}{4}$	$\frac{3}{4}$	$1\frac{1}{2}$
$2\frac{3}{4}$	$2\frac{2}{5}$	$\frac{2}{3}$

A. ⌊_⌋ x ⌊_⌋
$2\frac{1}{2} \times \frac{4}{5}$
____

B. ⌈‾⌉ x ⌈‾
____
____

C. [x]
____
____

D. □ x ‾⌉
____
____

E. _⌋ x ‾⌉
____
____

F. ⌈‾ x ⌊_
____
____

G. ⌊_⌋ x ⌈‾⌉
____
____

H. □ x]
____
____

I. ⌈‾⌉ x]
____
____

J. ‾⌉ x ⌊_
____
____

K. ⌈‾⌉ x [
____
____

L. Which two factors will make the greatest product? Write the factors and solve the equation.
____
____

M. Which two factors will make the smallest product? Write the factors and solve the equation.
____
____

Name ______________________________

Cooking for a Crowd

Use Marc's Crunchy Munchy recipe to solve the problems.

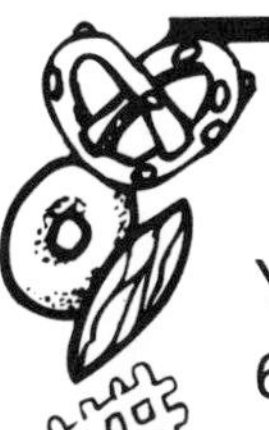

Crunchy Munchy for 8

You need:

6 ½ cups dry cereal

1 ¼ cups nuts

2 ¾ cups pretzel sticks

⅔ cup margarine

⅛ cup teriyaki sauce

1 ½ teaspoons garlic

Melt margarine. Mix with teriyaki sauce and garlic. Mix cereal, nuts, and pretzels. Pour sauce mixture over it. Bake in pan at 200° for 45 minutes.

1. How many cups of nuts would you need to make Crunchy Munchy for 16? ____________
2. How many cups of pretzel sticks would you need to make Crunchy Munchy for 24?

   ____
3. How many cups of margarine would you need to make Crunchy Munchy for 16?

   ____
4. Would 6 cups of pretzel sticks be enough for 16 servings? ____________

Complete the list of ingredients to make the servings shown.

5. 40 servings

   ______ cups dry cereal

   ______ cups nuts

   ______ cups pretzel sticks

   ______ cups margarine

   ______ cup teriyaki sauce

   ______ teaspoons garlic

6. 12 servings (Multiply by 1 ½.)

   ______ cups dry cereal

   ______ cups nuts

   ______ cups pretzel sticks

   ______ cup margarine

   ______ cup teriyaki sauce

   ______ teaspoons garlic

Name________________________________

Pattern Block Division

Cut out the pattern blocks. Use them to solve the problems.

A. How many $\frac{1}{3}$'s in 1? ______ $1 \div \frac{1}{3} =$ ______

B. How many $\frac{1}{2}$'s in 1? ______ $1 \div \frac{1}{2} =$ ______

C. How many $\frac{1}{6}$'s in $\frac{1}{3}$? ______ $\frac{1}{3} \div \frac{1}{6} =$ ______

D. How many $\frac{1}{6}$'s in $\frac{1}{2}$? ______ $\frac{1}{2} \div \frac{1}{6} =$ ______

E. How many $\frac{1}{3}$'s in 4? ______ $4 \div \frac{1}{3} =$ ______

F. How many $\frac{1}{2}$'s in 5? ______ $5 \div \frac{1}{2} =$ ______

G. How many $\frac{1}{2}$'s in $\frac{1}{2}$? ______ $\frac{1}{2} \div \frac{1}{2} =$ ______

H. How many $\frac{1}{3}$'s in 2? ______ $2 \div \frac{1}{3} =$ ______

I. How many $\frac{1}{6}$'s in $\frac{2}{3}$? ______ $\frac{2}{3} \div \frac{1}{6} =$ ______

J. How many $\frac{1}{2}$'s in 4? ______ $4 \div \frac{1}{2} =$ ______

K. How many $\frac{1}{3}$'s in $\frac{1}{3}$? ______ $\frac{1}{3} \div \frac{1}{3} =$ ______

L. How many $\frac{1}{6}$'s in 2? ______ $2 \div \frac{1}{6} =$ ______

M. How many $\frac{1}{3}$'s in 10? ______ $10 \div \frac{1}{3} =$ ______

N. How many $\frac{1}{2}$'s in 12? ______ $12 \div \frac{1}{2} =$ ______

O. How many $\frac{1}{3}$'s in 8? ______ $8 \div \frac{1}{3} =$ ______

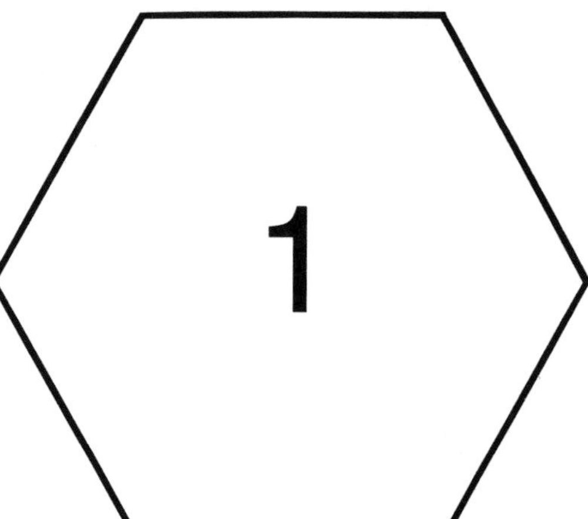

$\frac{1}{3}$

$\frac{1}{2}$

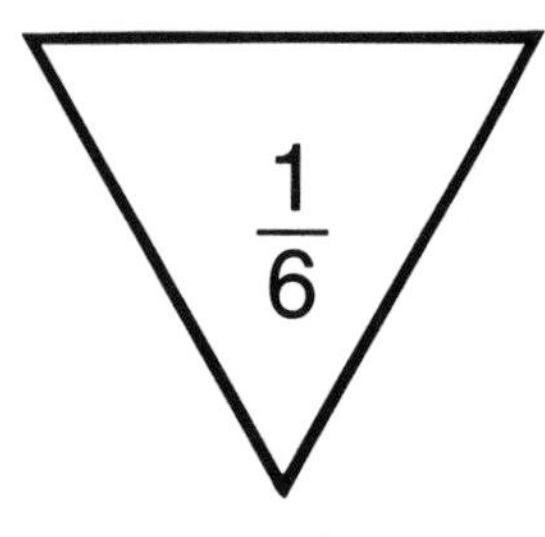

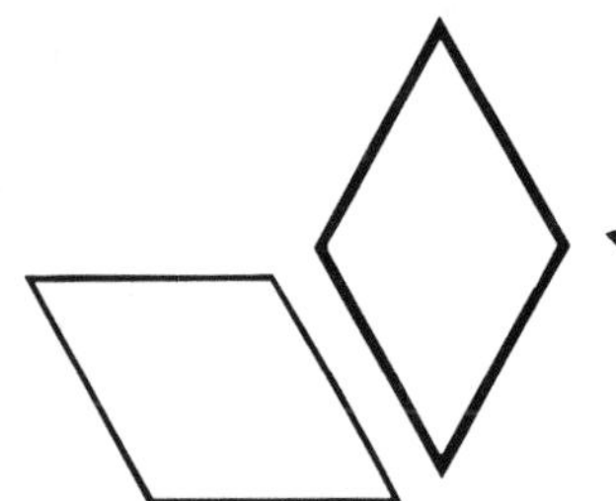

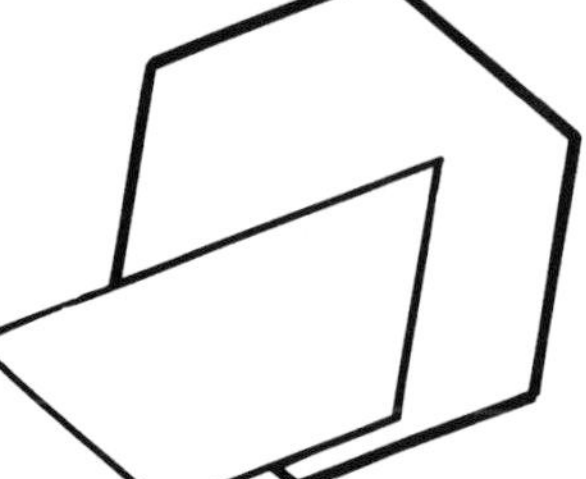

Ratios and Percents

Students will benefit greatly from the ratio and percent reinforcement and extension ideas described below and on page 50. Be sure to provide students with ample opportunities to work with manipulatives and complete several examples with your guidance. Provide students with time for conceptual understanding before proceeding through the more independent student activity pages (pages 51–56).

Be sure to point out how students may use their new skills in everyday life. For example, students can use their knowledge of ratios and percents when they calculate unit prices and analyze surveys. Help students observe the world around them and identify their own connections to ratios and percents.

CONCEPTS

The ideas and activities presented in this section will help students explore the following concepts:

- *understanding ratios*
- *solving proportions*
- *problem solving*
- *relating fractions and percents*
- *finding percents of numbers*
- *relating fractions, percents, and decimals*

WRITING ABOUT RATIOS

Writing Activity

Have students write and complete ratio sentences such as those below so that they make sense.

a. 2 gloves for 1 person, 6 gloves for _____ people (3)

b. 3 apples for the price of 2 oranges, 12 apples for the price of _____ oranges (8)

c. 2 balls for every 5 children, 10 balls for every _____ children (25)

Have each student make up five sentences. Have students exchange papers and solve each other's problems.

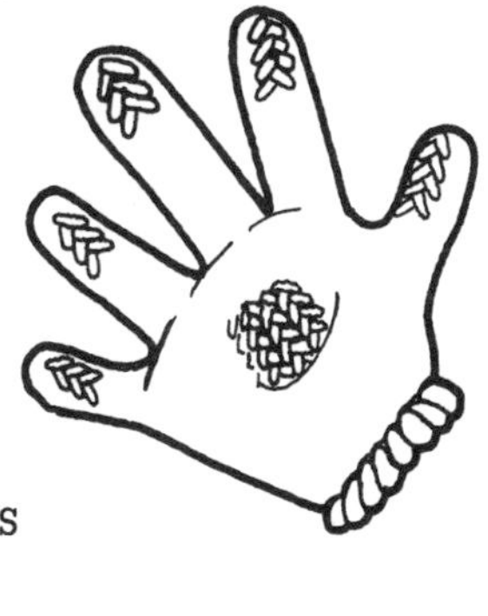

Bulletin Board

Pictured Percents

Distribute hundred square paper to each student. Have students color some squares on their papers. On index cards, have each student write a fraction, a decimal, and a percent matching the amount of squares colored in. Collect all hundred square papers and index cards and display them randomly on a bulletin board. Have students staple yarn lengths to connect each hundred square design to its matching index cards.

NAME THE RATIO

Class Activity

Write tables on the overhead such as the following:

x	10	15	20
y	18	27	36

a	24	32	40
b	18	24	30

Have students write the ratio for each table and give the next three equivalent ratios.

Answers:

x	5	25	30	35
y	9	45	54	63

a	8	48	56	64
b	6	36	42	48

DECIMAL DEFINITIONS

Writing Activity

In their journals, have students write definitions for *ratios; proportions; solving proportions;* and *relationships of fractions, decimals,* and *percents.*

PROPORTION PUZZLER

Class Activity

Have students write as many proportions as they can using the digits 2, 6, 8, and 24. (Possible answers: $\frac{2}{6} = \frac{8}{24}$; $\frac{2}{8} = \frac{6}{24}$; $\frac{6}{2} = \frac{24}{8}$; $\frac{6}{24} = \frac{2}{8}$; $\frac{8}{2} = \frac{24}{6}$; $\frac{8}{24} = \frac{2}{6}$; $\frac{24}{6} = \frac{8}{2}$; $\frac{24}{8} = \frac{6}{2}$)

FINDING PERCENTS USING CALCULATORS

Class Activity

Write the fraction $\frac{1}{4}$ on the overhead. Remind students that a fraction represents division (i.e., $\frac{1}{4}$ means "one divided by four"). Have students enter [1] [÷] [4] [=] in their calculators, write the decimal (answer), and then write the decimal as a percent (for example: $\frac{1}{4}$ = 0.25 = 25%). Have students use their calculators to find percent equivalents for $\frac{1}{2}$ (0.5; 50%), $\frac{3}{12}$ (0.25 = 25%), and $\frac{3}{8}$ (0.375 = 37.5%).

Homework

School-Home Connection

An Added Cost

Have students discuss the local sales tax with their families. Then students can search through newspapers or magazines to find 10 advertisements that contain prices. Students can work with their parents to calculate tax on the 10 items and then use those amounts to find the total cost of each item. Put the advertisements and papers on a bulletin board so students can compare prices.

Name ____

Making and Using Ratio Tables

Make a ratio table to help you solve each problem.

A. A can of 3 tennis balls costs $4. How much would it cost to buy 18 tennis balls?

____

tennis balls	3	6	9			
cost	$4					

B. Shelly uses 5 scoops of cocoa to make 2 mugs of hot chocolate. How many mugs can she make with 30 scoops of cocoa?

____

scoops of cocoa						
mugs of hot chocolate						

C. Carl pays 2 quarters to play 3 minutes of air hockey. How long can Carl play if he has 10 quarters?

____

quarters						
minutes of play						

D. It took Pam 5 minutes to solve 4 math problems. How long will it take Pam to solve 24 problems?

____

minutes						
math problems						

E. Tim can buy an 8-pack of markers for $5. He has $30. How many markers can he buy?

____

markers						
cost						

Name ____

Puzzle

X Marks the Spot

Solve for **x**. Shade in the answers in the box below. Your answers will form a design.

A. $\frac{5}{6} = \frac{\mathbf{x}}{24}$ x = ______ $\frac{1}{4} = \frac{\mathbf{x}}{20}$ x = ______ $\frac{9}{10} = \frac{\mathbf{x}}{50}$ x = ______

B. $\frac{2}{3} = \frac{\mathbf{x}}{18}$ x = ______ $\frac{3}{4} = \frac{\mathbf{x}}{20}$ x = ______ $\frac{4}{7} = \frac{\mathbf{x}}{28}$ x = ______

C. $\frac{3}{8} = \frac{\mathbf{x}}{48}$ x = ______ $\frac{5}{2} = \frac{\mathbf{x}}{10}$ x = ______ $\frac{1}{3} = \frac{\mathbf{x}}{30}$ x = ______

D. $\frac{7}{3} = \frac{\mathbf{x}}{18}$ x = ______ $\frac{7}{9} = \frac{\mathbf{x}}{72}$ x = ______ $\frac{8}{9} = \frac{\mathbf{x}}{36}$ x = ______

E. $\frac{2}{7} = \frac{\mathbf{x}}{49}$ x = ______ $\frac{5}{8} = \frac{\mathbf{x}}{64}$ x = ______ $\frac{9}{10} = \frac{\mathbf{x}}{70}$ x = ______

19	20		63	31
16	13	40	29	12
15	42	23	45	10
14	37	25	11	5
43	18	56	32	17

What is it? ____________

Name____

Riddle

An Unusual Timepiece

Complete each equation with a ratio or a percent. Use your answers to find a definition for "a unique timepiece."

A. $\frac{11}{100}$ = ______ A. $\frac{8}{100}$ = ______ A. $\frac{17}{100}$ = ______ A. $\frac{25}{100}$ = ______

A. $\frac{31}{100}$ = ______ E. $\frac{43}{100}$ = ______ E. $\frac{77}{100}$ = ______ I. $\frac{49}{100}$ = ______

I. $\frac{4}{100}$ = ______ O. $\frac{19}{100}$ = ______ O. $\frac{23}{100}$ = ______ W. $\frac{46}{100}$ = ______

G. $\frac{25}{100}$ = ______ T. $\frac{33}{100}$ = ______ D. $\frac{79}{100}$ = ______ T. 14% = ______

L. 67% = ______ M. 58% = ______ C. 53% = ______ C. 28% = ______

H. 12% = ______ H. 71% = ______ N. 17% = ______ T. 39% = ______

S. 84% = ______ T. 47% = ______

D. 91% = ______ G. 5% = ______

T. 75% = ______

L. 2% = ______

___ 11%   ___ 46% ___ 8% ___ $\frac{75}{100}$ ___ $\frac{28}{100}$ ___ $\frac{71}{100}$ ___ 79% ___ 19% ___ $\frac{5}{100}$

___ 49% ___ $\frac{84}{100}$ ___ 17%   ___ $\frac{91}{100}$ ___ 23% ___ 25%   ___ $\frac{47}{100}$ ___ $\frac{12}{100}$ ___ 25% ___ $\frac{39}{100}$

___ $\frac{53}{100}$ ___ 31% ___ $\frac{17}{100}$ ___ 33% ___ 43% ___ $\frac{2}{100}$ ___ $\frac{67}{100}$ ___ $\frac{14}{100}$ ___ 4% ___ $\frac{58}{100}$ ___ 77% .

Name______________________________________

Puzzling Problems

Find the percent problems. Use your answers to solve the puzzle.

ACROSS

A. 10% of 100 = _______

B. 20% of 125 = _______

D. 33 ⅓% of 135 = _______

E. 66 ⅔% of 75 = _______

F. 50% of 130 = _______

G. 15% of 500 = _______

H. 5% of 16,000 = _______

I. 25% of 360 = _______

J. 10% of 150 = _______

L. 20% of 150 = _______

M. 50% of 90 = _______

N. 50% of 1,120 = _______

P. 25% of 280 = _______

Q. 50% of 160 = _______

R. 20% of 450 = _______

DOWN

A. 20% of 75 = _______

B. 40% of 50 = _______

C. 50% of 750 = _______

D. 5% of 8,000 = _______

E. 10% of 550 = _______

F. 25% of 2,500 = _______

G. 66 ⅔% of 105 = _______

H. 50% of 170 = _______

I. 25% of 380 = _______

J. 1% of 10,000 = _______

K. 50% of 450 = _______

L. 25% of 140 = _______

M. 80% of 50 = _______

O. 80% of 750 = _______

P. 50% of 140 = _______

Q. 25% of 340 = _______

Name ____________________

Making the Grade

Find the percentage for each student's test. Write it beside the word "Score." Then give each test a grade based on the scale shown to the right.

90–100	A
80–89	B
70–79	C
60–69	D

1. Erica 18/20
   Score: _____
   Grade: _____

2. Lamont 20/25
   Score: _____
   Grade: _____

3. Cathy 9/12
   Score: _____
   Grade: _____

4. Sara 48/50
   Score: _____
   Grade: _____

5. Rick 17/25
   Score: _____
   Grade: _____

6. Matthew 12/15
   Score: _____
   Grade: _____

7. Judith 23/25
   Score: _____
   Grade: _____

8. Uma 30/40
   Score: _____
   Grade: _____

9. Penny 66/75
   Score: _____
   Grade: _____

10. Hector 17/20
    Score: _____
    Grade: _____

11. Mary 46/50
    Score: _____
    Grade: _____

12. Holly 81/90
    Score: _____
    Grade: _____

13. Victoria 38/50
    Score: _____
    Grade: _____

14. Ed 186/200
    Score: _____
    Grade: _____

15. Ben 33/55
    Score: _____
    Grade: _____

Name ____

Cross-Out

Cross out the box in each row that does not belong. The letters in those boxes, when written in order, will answer the following question:

What did the farmer raise in the family room?

1.	S 50%	T $\frac{55}{100}$	U $\frac{1}{2}$	V 0.5	W
2.	F 25%	G $\frac{25}{100}$	H $\frac{1}{5}$	I 0.25	J
3.	B 30%	C $\frac{30}{100}$	D $\frac{3}{10}$	E 0.33	F
4.	V 15%	W $\frac{5}{100}$	X $\frac{3}{20}$	Y 0.15	Z
5.	E 12.5%	F $\frac{125}{1000}$	G $\frac{1}{8}$	H 0.125	I
6.	M 60%	N $\frac{6}{100}$	O $\frac{3}{5}$	P 0.6	Q
7.	B 80%	C $\frac{80}{100}$	D $\frac{3}{8}$	E 0.8	F
8.	K 5%	L $\frac{5}{100}$	M $\frac{1}{20}$	N 0.05	O
9.	W 75%	X $\frac{85}{100}$	Y $\frac{17}{20}$	Z 0.85	A

___ ___ ___ ___ ___ ___ ___ ___ ___

1 2 3 4 5 6 7 8 9

Geometry

Students will benefit greatly from the stimulating geometry reinforcement and extension ideas described below and on page 58. Be sure to provide students with ample opportunities to work with manipulatives and complete several examples with your guidance. Provide students with time for conceptual understanding before proceeding through the more independent student activity pages (pages 59–64). Be sure to point out how students may use their new skills in everyday life. For example, students will use their knowledge of geometry when they construct geometric figures or designs or when they use symmetry in art. Help students observe the world around them and identify their own connections to geometry.

CONCEPTS

The ideas and activities presented in this section will help students explore the following concepts:

- *naming quadrilaterals*
- *naming triangles (acute, right, scalene, equilateral, isosceles)*
- *measuring triangles*
- *using coordinate graphs*
- *defining geometry terms*
- *defining congruent and similar figures*

SOLID FIGURE IDENTIFICATION

Group Activity

Brainstorm with students geometric shapes of real-life objects. For example, a cereal box is an example of a rectangular prism; a funnel is an example of a cone; and a mug is an example of a cylinder. Next, provide students with magazines and have them cut out geometric-shaped objects such as those they mentioned. Finally, students can create collages showing one specific geometric shape (i.e., rectangular prisms).

Group Activity

Flips, Slides, and Turns

Have students work in pairs. One student draws a triangle or a quadrilateral on a geoboard dot paper grid. The other student draws the same figure, but flipped, slid, or turned on another geoboard dot paper grid, using a different colored pencil or marker. The pairs must decide and agree upon how the first figure was flipped, slid, or turned to reach its location in the second figure. Students write the description of movement below the pair of geoboard dot paper grids. Then they switch roles and repeat.

Art Project

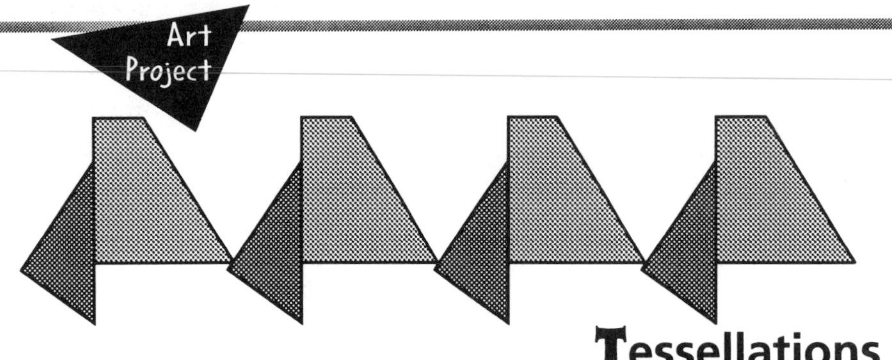

Tessellations

Provide each student with a plain sheet of paper, a 1 ½″ square piece of index card, scissors, and clear tape. Have each student cut a section from one side of the square card and tape it to the opposite side to form a tessellating figure. Then students trace the figures, one beside the other, to form tessellating designs. Allow time for students to color their completed tessellation designs. Display finished products on a bulletin board.

Class Activity

SYMMETRY

Have students write their first and last names using capital letters. Then have them draw lines of symmetry through any letters that they can. Next, challenge students to find words that have horizontal or vertical lines of symmetry. (Example: horizontal—BIKE; vertical—MOMMY)

GEOMETRY DEFINITIONS

On the board, list terms you want students to learn (i.e., *triangles—acute, right, scalene*). In their journals, have students write definitions for the terms. They could also draw pictures to represent each term. If some students are having trouble, divide students into pairs. Have the pairs write definitions together. Just talking things through really helps some students.

COMPLEMENTARY AND SUPPLEMENTARY ANGLES

Game

Have students play this game in groups of three. Player A names an angle less than 90°. Player B names the complementary angle, and Player C names the supplementary angle. Players switch roles and repeat.

SCHOOL-HOME CONNECTION

Homework

Packaging Party

Have students classify the objects in their refrigerators into groups of solid figures such as cylinders, cubes, rectangular prisms, and combination figures. Then students may use estimation to determine which type of solid figure is most used for food packaging (i.e., liquid—cylinders; solids—rectangular prisms).

Name ______________________________________

Quadrilateral Riddles

Solve each riddle. Then draw it on the geoboard dot paper grids. Use the Word Bank to help you.

Word Bank

kite parallelogram rectangle rhombus square trapezoid

1. I have 2 pairs of parallel sides and 2 pairs of congruent angles. I have no right angles. What am I?

   ____

2. I have only one pair of parallel sides. What am I?

   ____

3. I have 2 pairs of parallel sides. All 4 of my sides are the same length, but I have no right angles. What am I?

   ____

4. I have 2 pairs of parallel sides. Each pair of sides is a different length. All 4 of my angles are right angles. What am I?

   ____

5. I have 2 pairs of touching sides the same length. None of my angles are right angles. What am I?

   ____

6. I have 2 pairs of parallel sides, and all of my sides are the same length. All of my angles have the same measure. What am I?

   ____

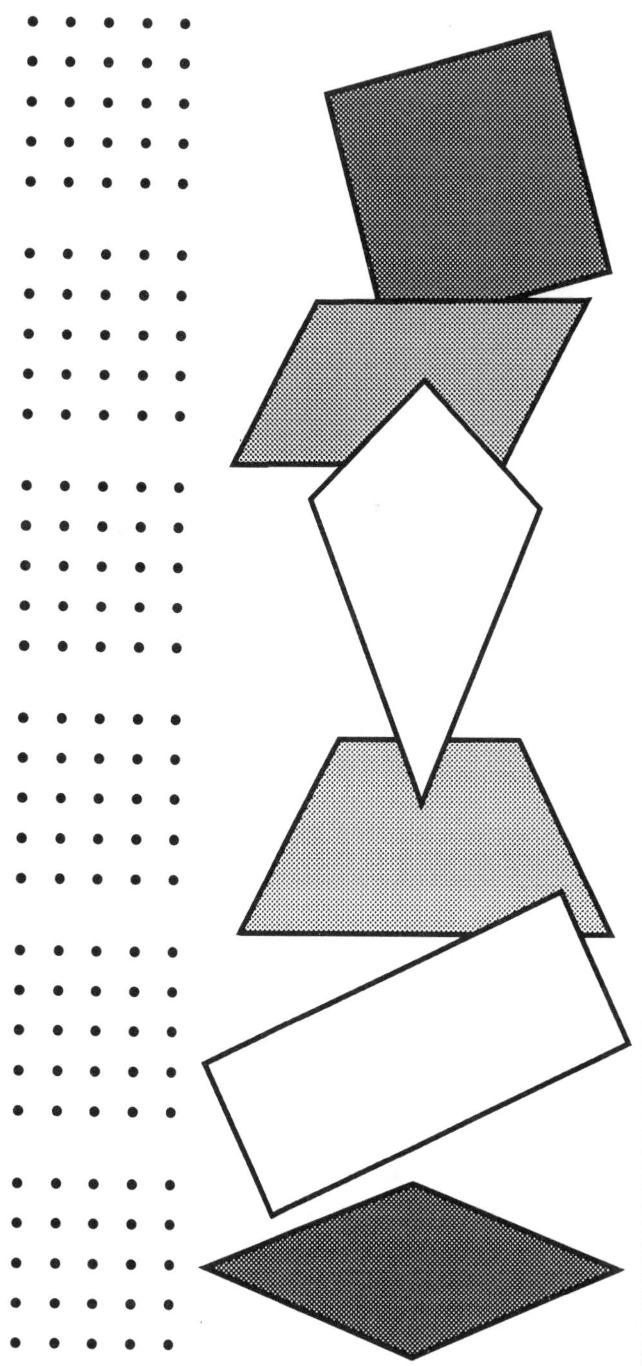

Name ______________________________

Bits and Pieces

The angles below can be combined to form four triangles. Use the letters to name each triangle.

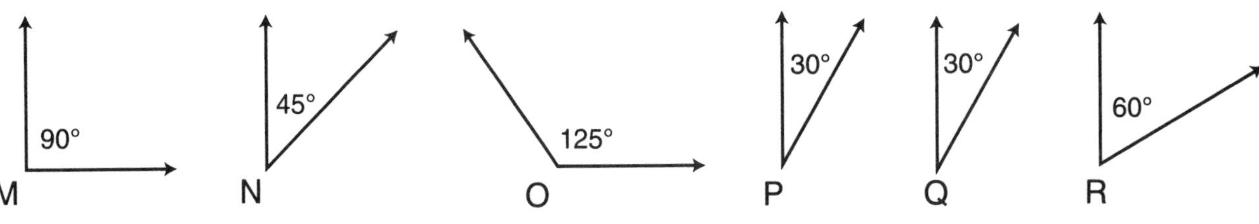

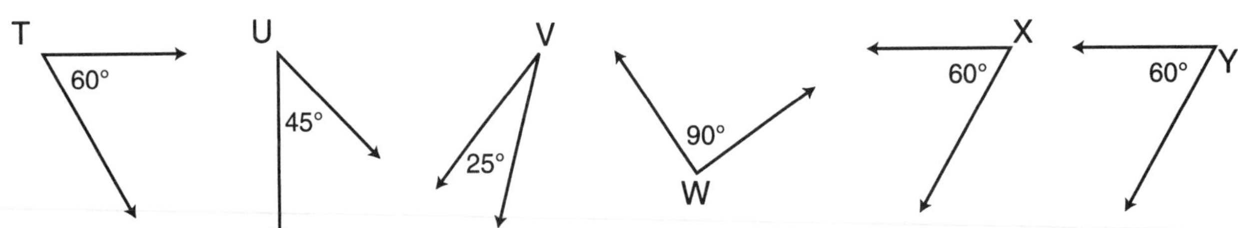

Triangle 1: ________

Triangle 2: ________

Triangle 3: ________

Triangle 4: ________

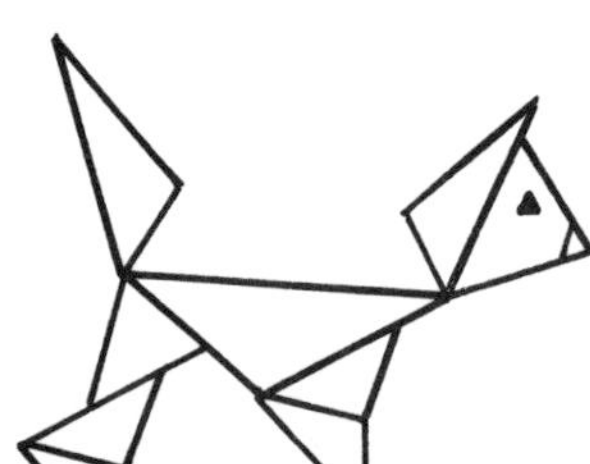

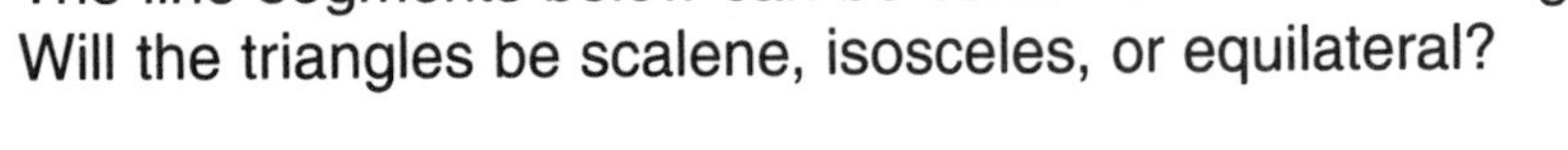

The line segments below can be combined to form triangles. Will the triangles be scalene, isosceles, or equilateral?

Triangle 5:

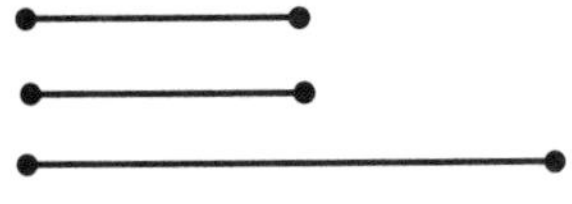

____

Triangle 6:

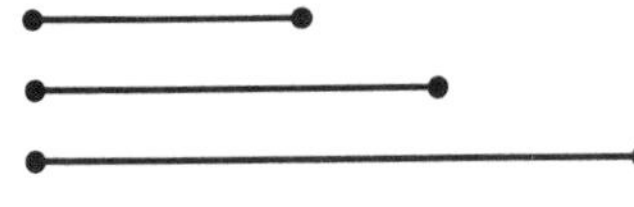

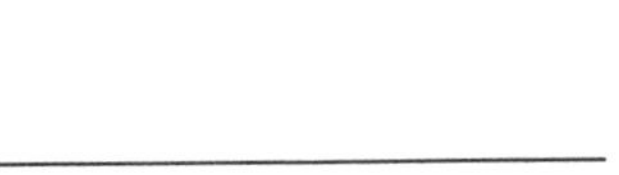

____

Triangle 7:

____

Triangle 8:

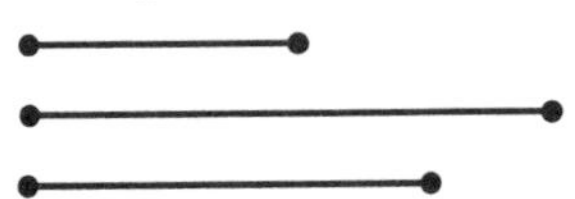

____

Triangle 9:

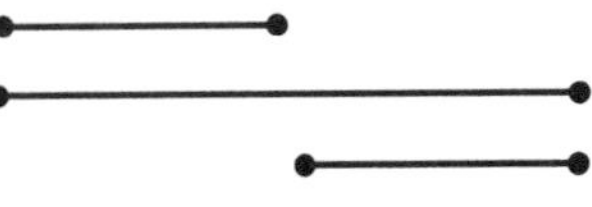

____

Name____

Riddle

Angling for an Answer

Measure each angle. Use your answers and the code to solve the following riddle:

What is black and white and read all over?

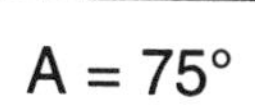

A = 75°
A = 110°
E = 95°
E = 20°
N = 150°
P = 45°
P = 130°
R = 90°
S = 55°
W = 40°

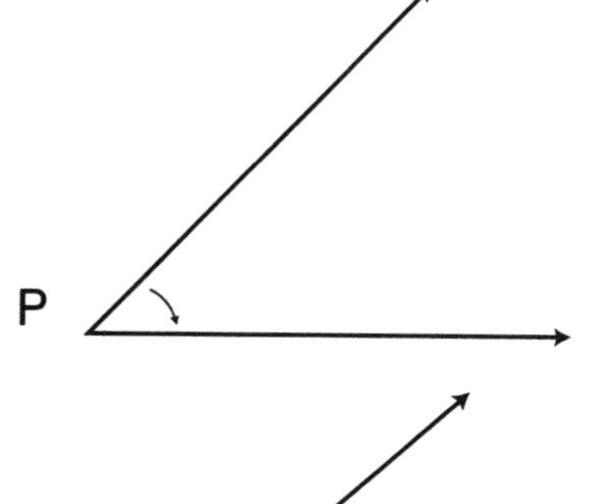

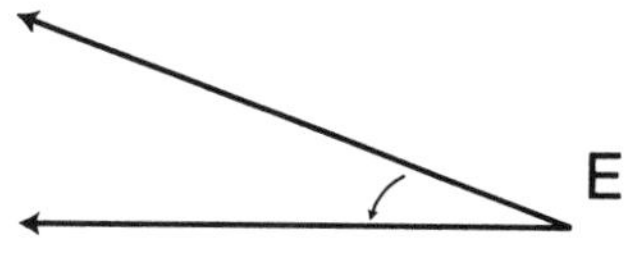

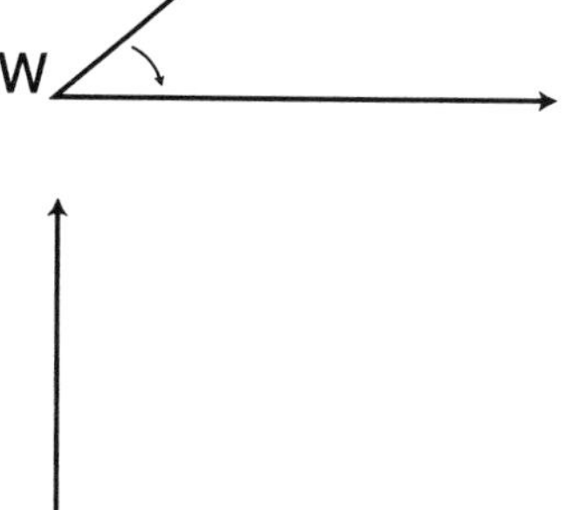

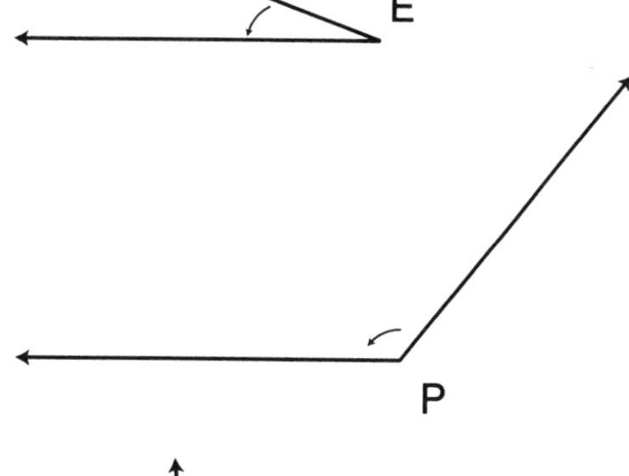

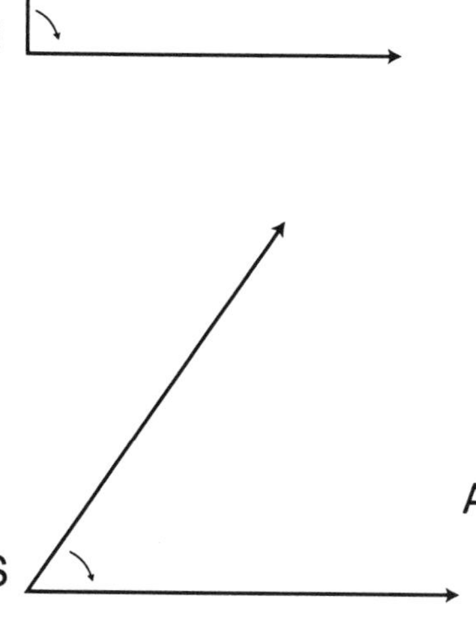

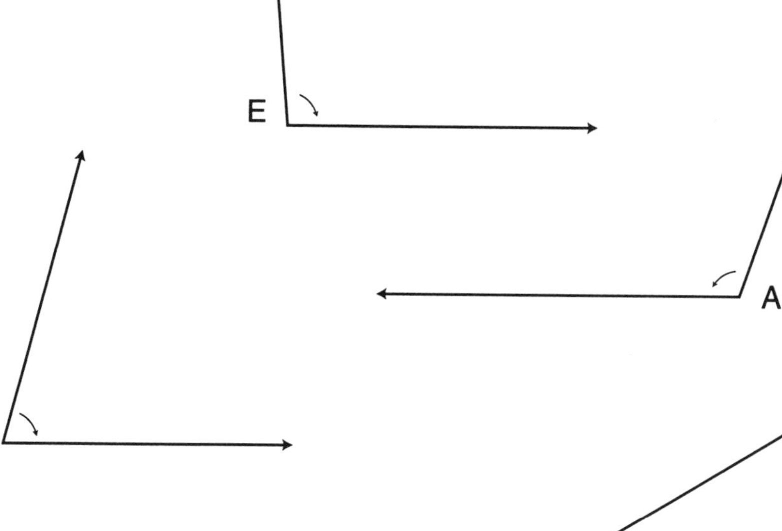

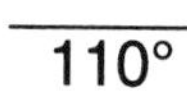

____ 110°

____ 150° ____ 20° ____ 40° ____ 55° ____ 45° ____ 75° ____ 130° ____ 95° ____ 90°

Name____

Congruent or Similar?

Decide if the figures below are congruent or similar.

If they are congruent, color the figures yellow.

If they are similar, color the figures blue.

If they are not congruent or similar, color the figures red.

A.

B.

C.

D.

E.

Name ____

Puzzle

Crossword Puzzle Jeopardy

Write the clues for each word in the crossword puzzle below.
You may draw pictures or diagrams to help.

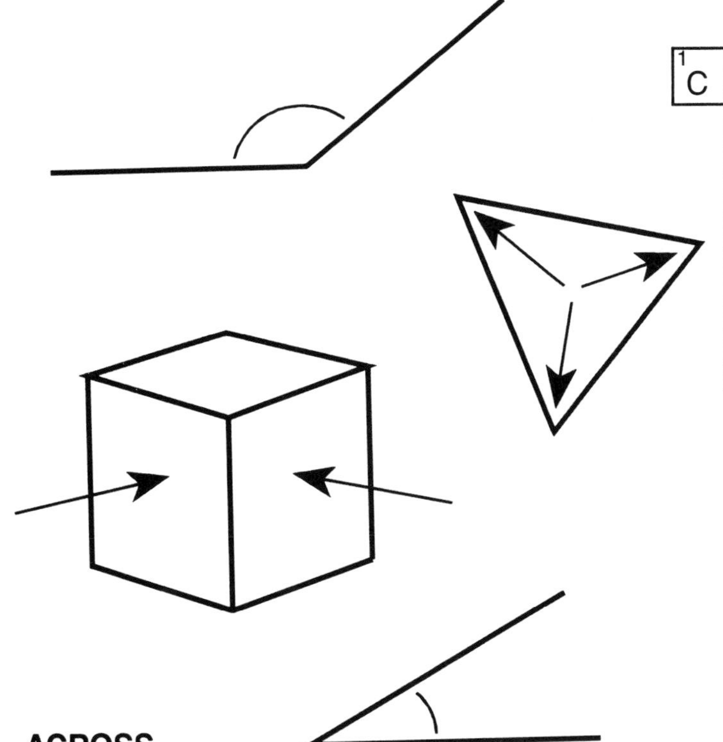

1 C	2 O	N	G	R	U	E	N	T			
	B										
	T										
	U			3 E							
	4 S	L	I	D	E			5 F	L	I	P
	E			G				A			
			6 V	E	7 R	T	I	C	E	8 S	
					I			E		I	
			9 A	N	G	L	E			M	
					H					I	
		10 A	C	U	T	E				L	
										A	
										R	

ACROSS

1. ______________________________
4. ______________________________
5. ______________________________
6. ______________________________
9. ______________________________
10. ______________________________

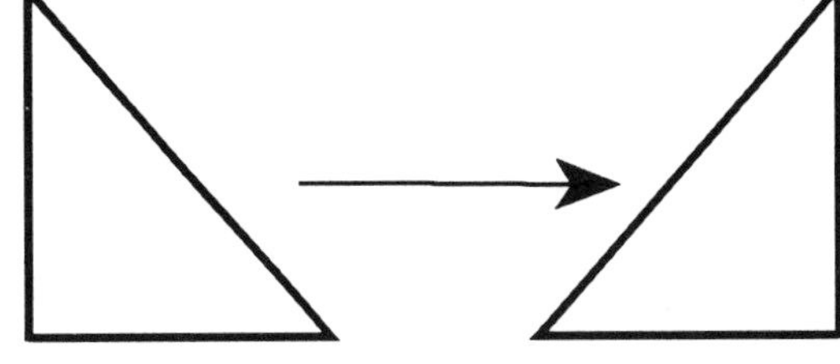

DOWN

2. ______________________________
3. ______________________________
5. ______________________________
7. ______________________________
8. ______________________________

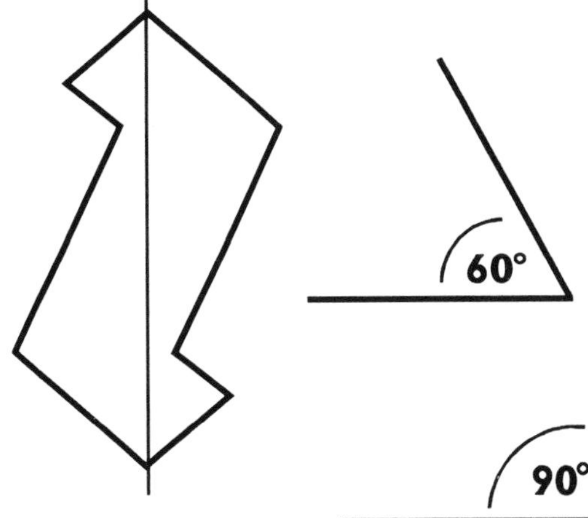

Name____

Euler's Law

Complete the table to learn about Euler's Law.

Space Figure	Vertices	Faces	Sum of vertices and faces	Edges
1.				
2.				
3.				
4.				
5.				
6.				
7.				

What do you notice about the sum of the faces and vertices and the number of edges in each figure?

____

____

Perimeter, Area, and Volume

Students will benefit greatly from the perimeter, area, and volume reinforcement and extension ideas described below and on pages 66 and 67. Be sure to provide students with ample opportunities to work with manipulatives and complete several examples with your guidance. Provide students with time for conceptual understanding before proceeding through the more independent student activity pages (pages 68–74). Don't hesitate to point out how students may use their new skills in everyday life. Students will use their knowledge of perimeter, area, and volume when they estimate and calculate fencing needed for a yard, or the amount of cereal that will fit into a plastic container. Help students observe the world around them and identify their own connections to perimeter, area, and volume.

Perimeter, area, and volume concepts also have natural connections to other mathematics concepts such as operations with whole numbers, decimals, and fractions.

CONCEPTS

The ideas and activities presented in this section will help students explore the following concepts:

- *finding perimeters of polygons*
- *finding circumferences of circles*
- *finding areas of quadrilaterals*
- *finding areas of triangles*
- *finding surface areas*
- *finding volume*
- *problem solving*

STRING PERIMETERS

Class Activity

Have students use string to find the perimeters of standard and non-standard objects. Students begin by wrapping string around objects, then cutting the string where the start and stop points meet. Students then use centimeter or inch rulers to measure their strings. This gives students the perimeters of the objects. Use this as a discussion of what perimeter actually is.

Class Demonstration

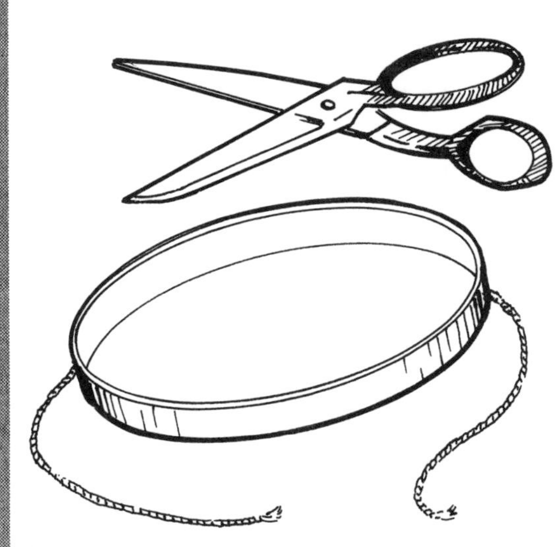

Pi (π)

Have students "prove" pi. Provide each student with a round lid, scissors, and a piece of string. Make sure students note that lids around the room are different sizes. Have students wrap their strings around the perimeters of the lids and cut exactly where the ends meet the beginnings. Then have students count the number of times they can stretch their strings across the diameters of their lids. Have the students share their answers. As student after student says, "a little more than 3 times," you can tell them that it is pi (π) times—$22/7$, or 3.14—every time.

ESTIMATING AREA OF NON-STANDARD SHAPES

Group Activity

Have students use graph paper to estimate the area of their hands. Students work in pairs and trace each other's hands. Students estimate the area of their hands by first counting all of the wholly-used squares, and then by counting all of the partially-used squares and dividing that total by two. Students may wish to compare their hands palm-to-palm to check their estimates.

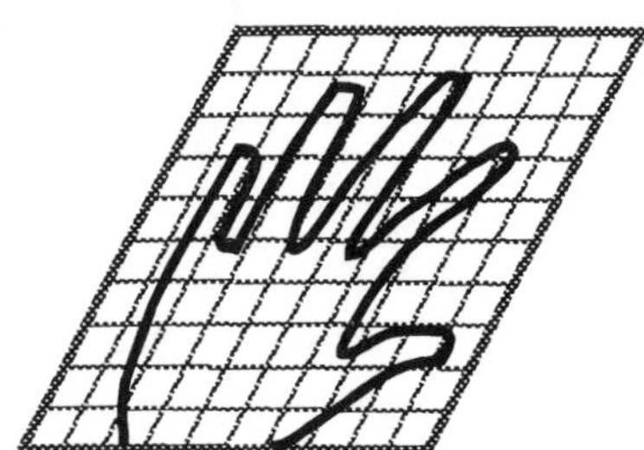

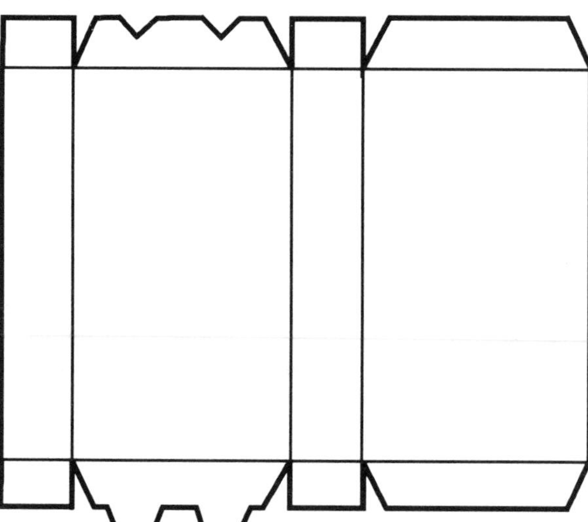

SURFACE AREA CEREAL BOXES

Class Activity

Have students bring in empty cereal boxes. Show students how to break apart the boxes so that all six faces of each box can be measured. Provide rulers and have students find the area of each of the six faces on each box. (Encourage students to notice that there are three pairs of equal faces. Therefore, only three faces need to be found.) Then have students add the areas of all six faces to find the total surface area of each cereal box.

Manipulative Activity

Same Area, Different Perimeter

Give students grid paper. On the grid paper, have students make as many different-shaped rectangles as they can that have an area of 24 square units. Have students write the perimeter of each rectangle they made. Invite students to make observations about their rectangles. (For example, rectangles become longer as they get narrower.) Display the grid papers on a bulletin board so that students can see that even though rectangles can have the same area, their perimeters can be different.

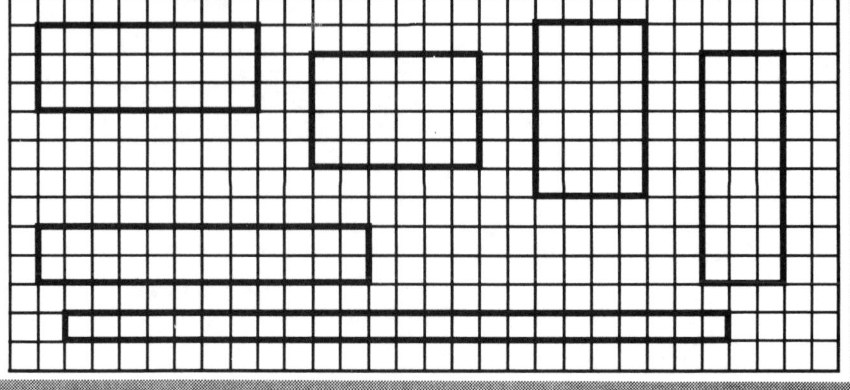

Manipulative Activity

LET'S COMPARE

This activity is a great way to show visual learners the difference between surface area and volume. Provide students with connecting cubes. Have them make rectangular prisms using the cubes. Tell them to count the cubes along each of the outside faces to find the surface area. To find the volume, have students multiply the number of cubes in one layer (length times width) by the number of layers.

ESTIMATED SURFACE AREA HUNT

Game

Students work in small groups. Each group is assigned to find as many rectangular prisms whose surface areas range between 800 cm^2 and 1000 cm^2 as it can. Provide students with a centimeter ruler and a 5-minute time limit. Students list the objects they find. After five minutes, students share and compare lists. The team with the most objects, whose estimates actually fall into the appointed range, wins the game.

VOLUME FUN

Class Demonstration

Do the following demonstration to have students use their critical thinking skills to estimate volume: Fill two identical jars—one with centimeter square units (A) and one with two-centimeter connecting cubes (B). Make sure students understand that the volume of each cube in jar B is four times that of each cube in jar A. On pieces of paper, have students estimate the number of cubes in each jar. Then have students estimate their volumes. When everyone is done, discuss students' findings. (Students should estimate that jar A contains about 4 times as many cubes as jar B, but their volumes should be equal.)

WHAT'S THE DIFFERENCE?

Writing Activity

In their journals, have students compare and contrast surface area and volume giving two examples of when each one would be used. (Possible comparisons: surface area is measured in square units; volume is measured in cubic units. The calculation methods are different. Surface area measures the outside, such as the amount of wrapping paper needed to cover a gift box. Volume measures the inside, such as the amount of dominoes that might fit inside a gift box.)

Homework

School-Home Connection

"Ad" and Measure

Have students look through newspapers to find advertisements for wall-to-wall carpeting. Tell students to use yardsticks or tape measures to measure in yards the length and width of a room in their home. Remind students that this number will most likely be a decimal or a fraction. Tell students to multiply to find the area of the room in square yards. Then students' families can work together to calculate the total cost of the advertised carpeting.

Name____

Riddle

All Around the Shapes

The perimeter of each shape below is given. Find the length of one side. (Hint: All sides of each shape are the same length.) Use your answers to break the code and answer the following question:

Who was the first female in space?

A.

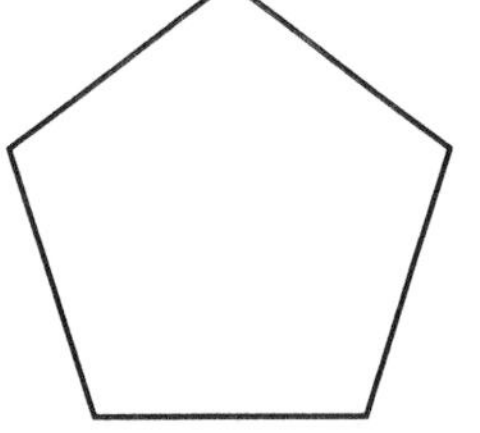

P = 35.5 in.

S = ____________

E.

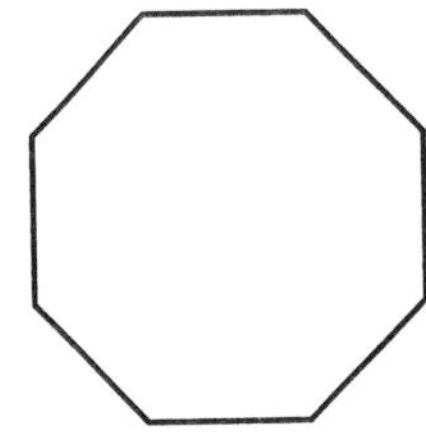

P = 30.4 in.

S = ____________

Y.

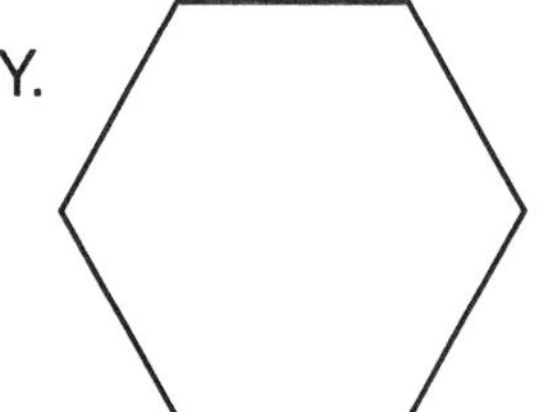

P = 24.54 in.

S = ____________

D.

P = 18.52 in.

S = ____________

I.

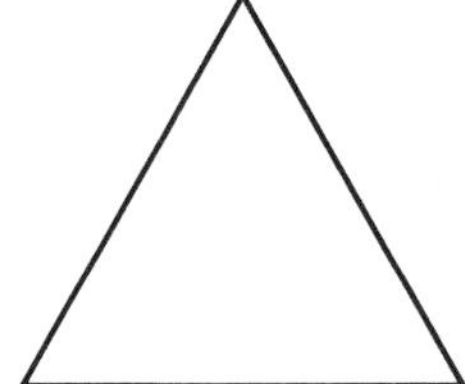

P = 10.05 in.

S = ____________

R.

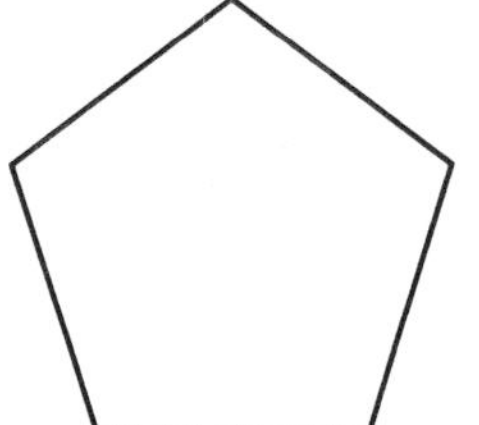

P = 26.25 in.

S = ____________

S.

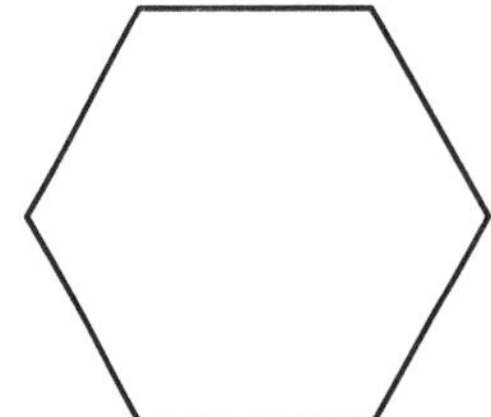

P = 24.75 in.

S = ____________

L.

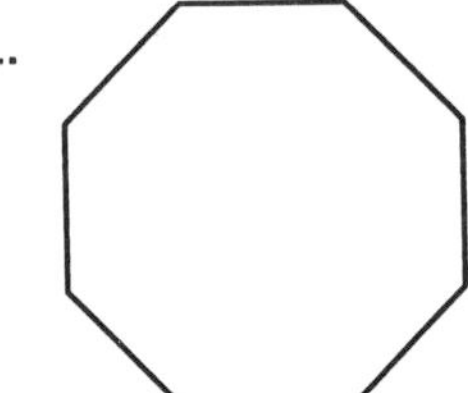

P = 49.6 in.

S = ____________

____	____	____	____	____		____	____	____	____
4.125 in.	7.1 in.	6.2 in.	6.2 in.	4.09 in.		5.25 in.	3.35 in.	4.63 in.	3.8 in.

Name ______________________________

A Riddle Rainy Riddle

Find the circumference of each circle below. Use πd or $2\pi r$. (Hint: $\pi = 3.14$) Match your answers to break the code and solve the following riddle:

What goes up when the rain comes down?

E.

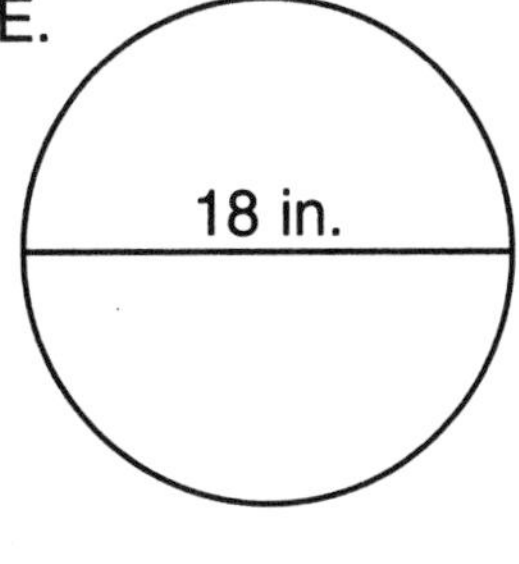

____

R.

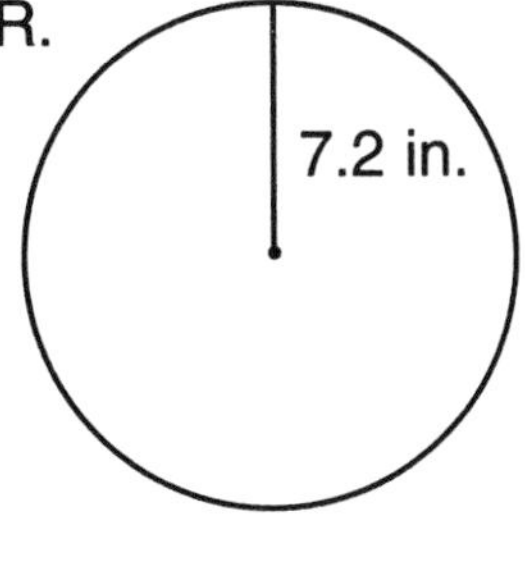

____

N.

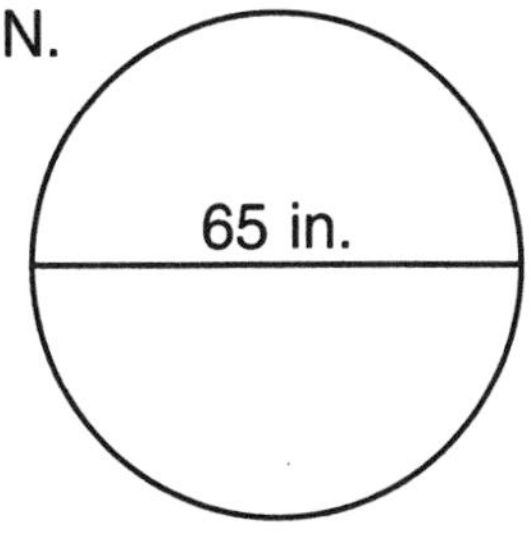

____

L.

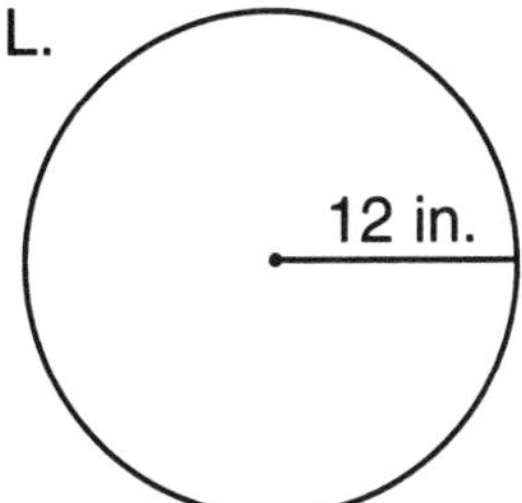

____

U.

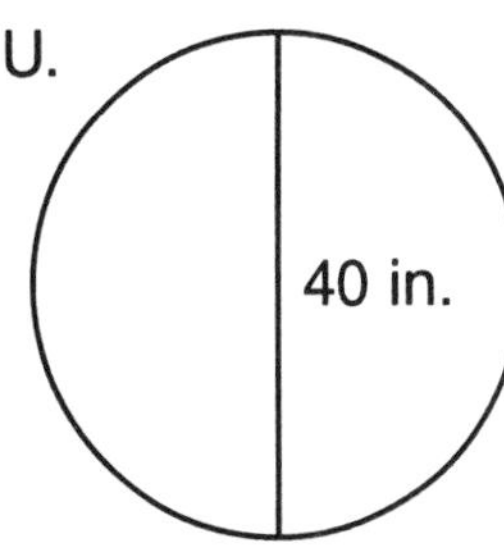

____

A.

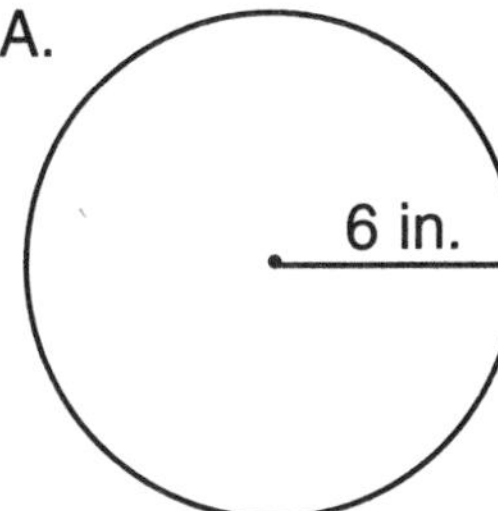

____

A.

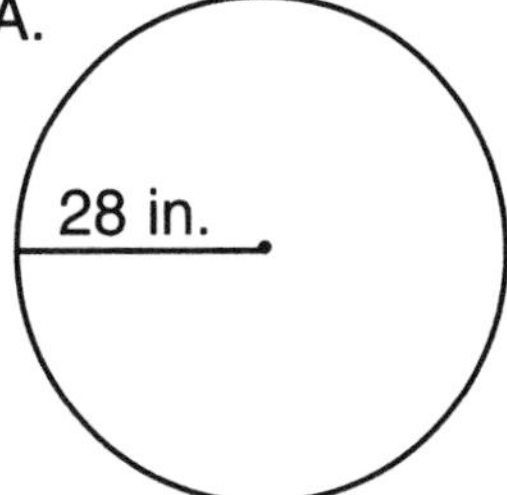

____

B.

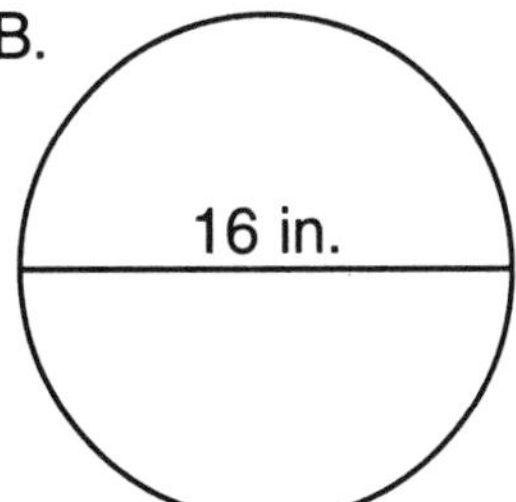

____

M.

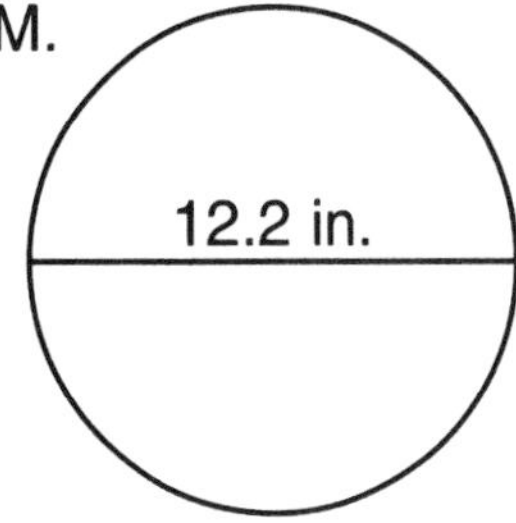

____

L.

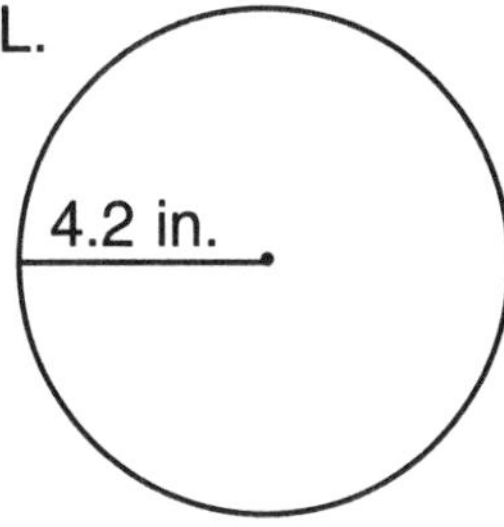

____

___	___		___	___	___	___	___	___	___	___
175.84 in.	204.1 in.		125.6 in.	38.308 in.	50.24 in.	45.216 in.	56.52 in.	75.36 in.	26.376 in.	37.68 in.

Name____

Puzzle

Area Design

Use A = l x w or A = b x h to find the area of each shape below. Shade in the sections that contain your answers to find a hidden letter.

What is it? __________

1. 18 ft. 6 ft.

A = ______________

2. 28 ft.

12 ft.

A = ______________

3. 25 ft.

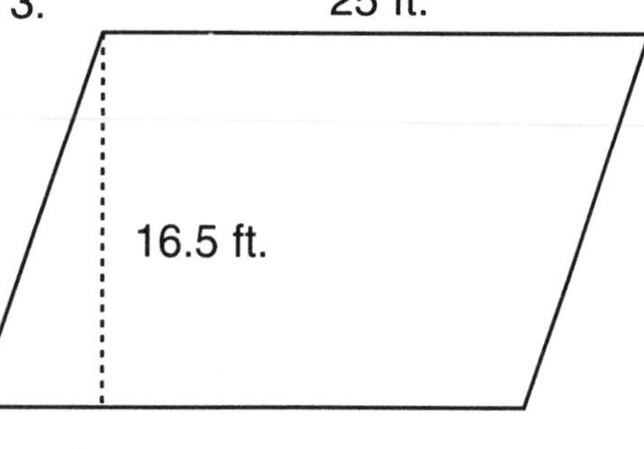

A = ______________

4. 12 ft.

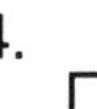

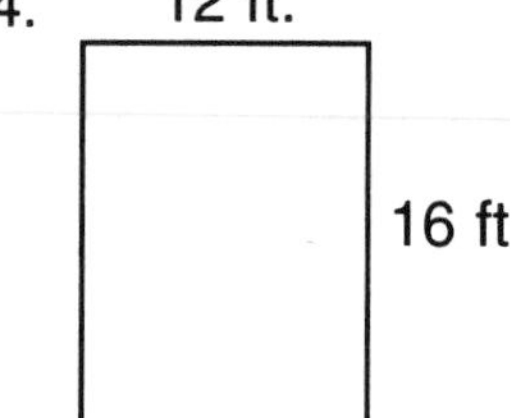

16 ft.

A = ______________

5. 10 ft.

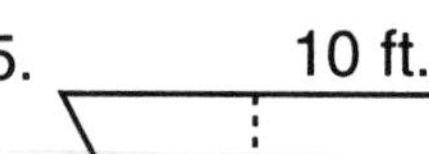

5.2 ft.

A = ______________

6. 30 ft.

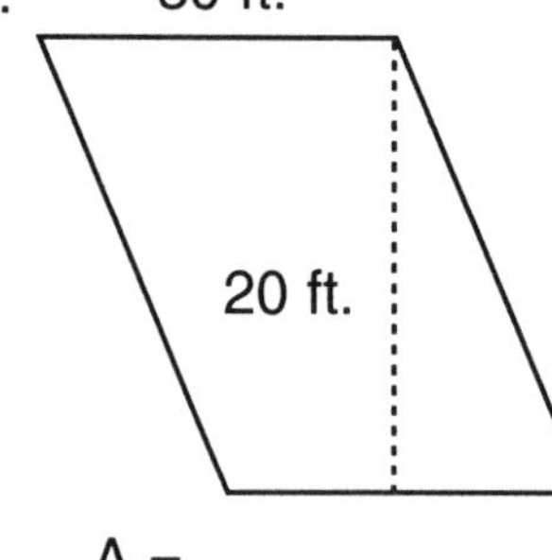

A = ______________

7. 1.8 ft.

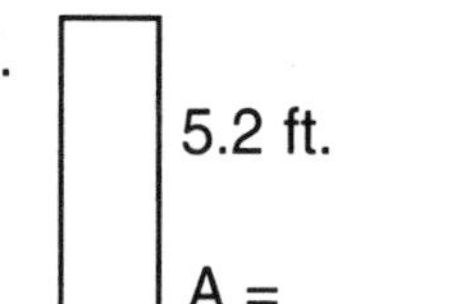

5.2 ft.

A = ______________

8. 17.1 ft.

6.8 ft.

A = ______________

9. 12.3 ft.

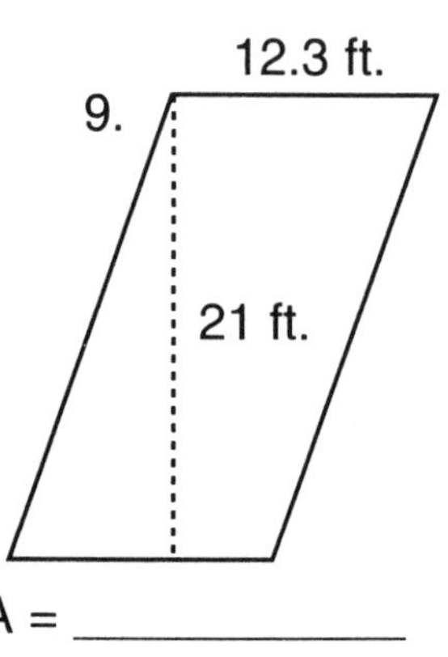

A = ______________

660 $ft.^2$	300 $ft.^2$	500 $ft.^2$	600 $ft.^2$	700 $ft.^2$	900 $ft.^2$	485 $ft.^2$
8.74 $ft.^2$	7.94 $ft.^2$	9.36 $ft.^2$	10.36 $ft.^2$	412.5 $ft.^2$	512.3 $ft.^2$	8.36 $ft.^2$
114.26 $ft.^2$	116.28 $ft.^2$	258.3 $ft.^2$	108 $ft.^2$		336 $ft.^2$	436 $ft.^2$
192 $ft.^2$	154 $ft.^2$	254 $ft.^2$	92 $ft.^2$	74 $ft.^2$	14 $ft.^2$	52 $ft.^2$

Name ________________________________

"Tri" It!

Find the area of each triangle below. Use A = ½bh.

1.

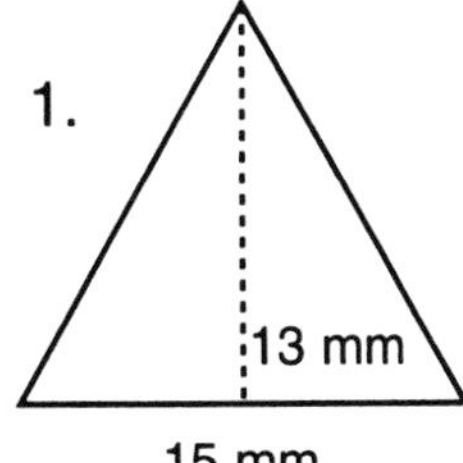

A = __________

2.

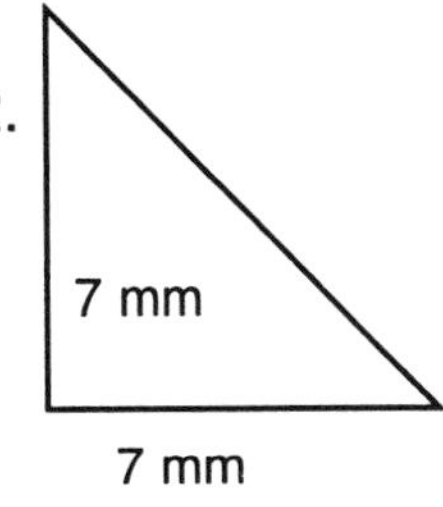

A = __________

3.

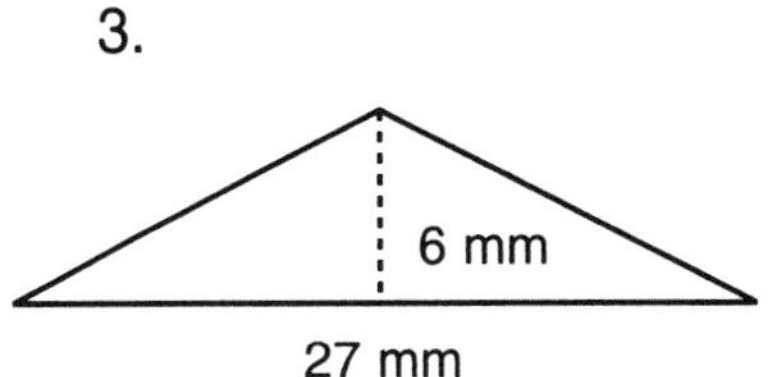

A = __________

4.

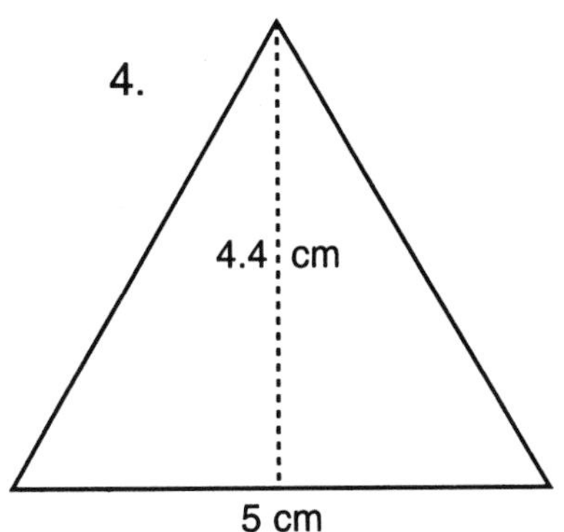

A = __________

5.

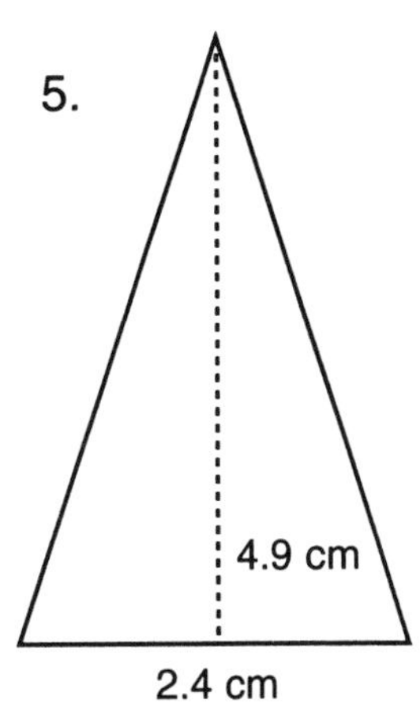

A = __________

6.

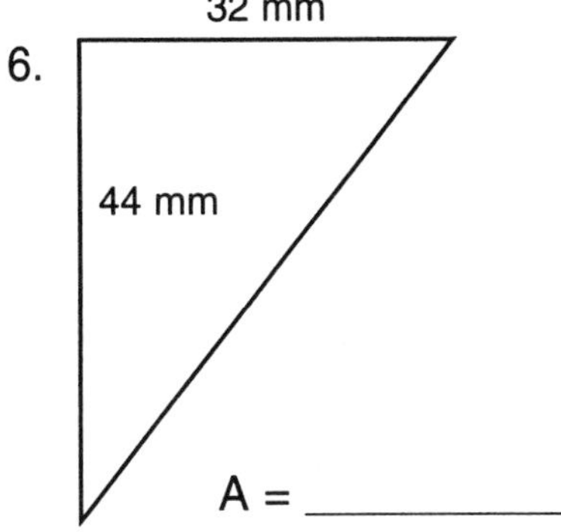

A = __________

7.

32 mm

16 mm

A = __________

8.

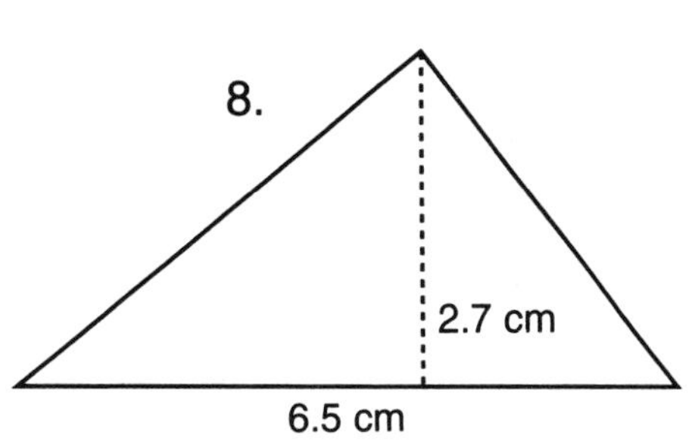

A = __________

9.

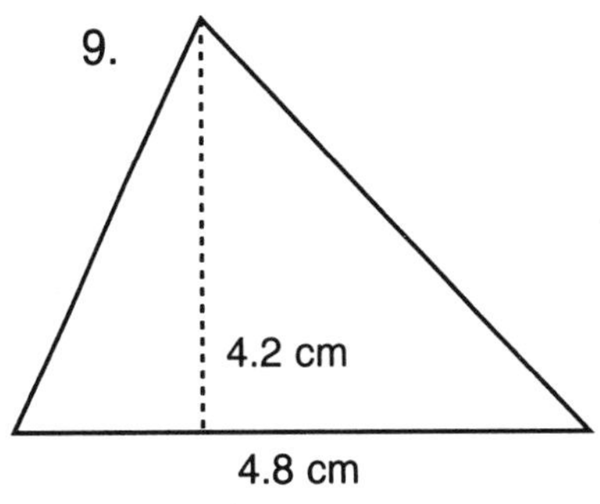

A = __________

Name___________________________________

Wrap It

How much wrapping paper is needed to wrap each box below? To find out, find the surface area for each box.

A.

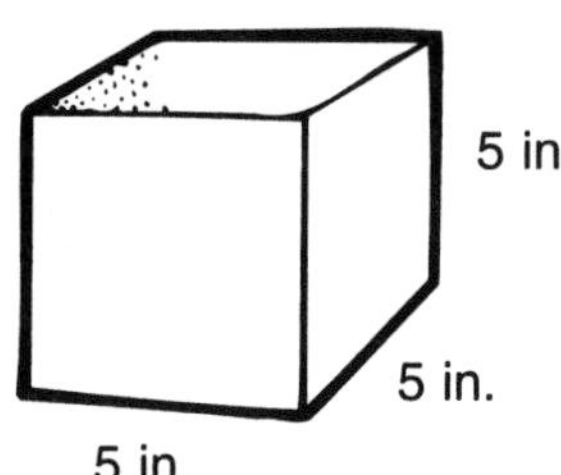

SA = __________

B.

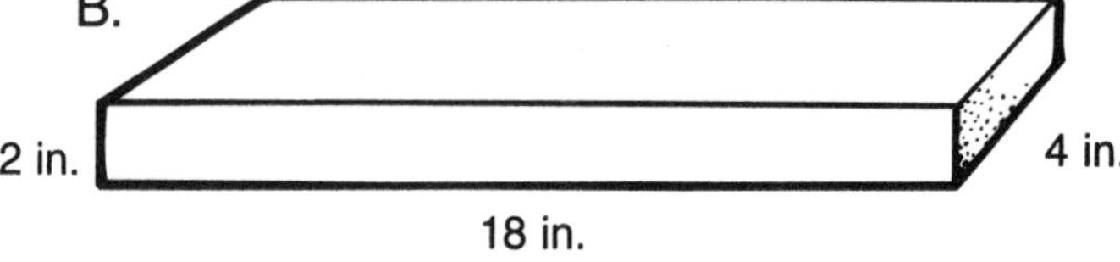
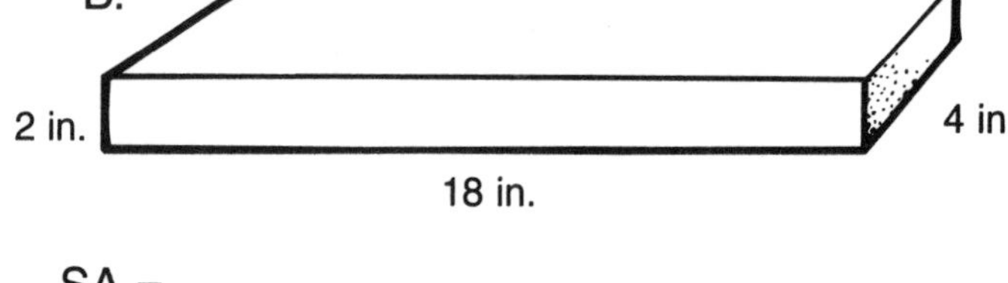

SA = __________

C.

SA = __________

D.

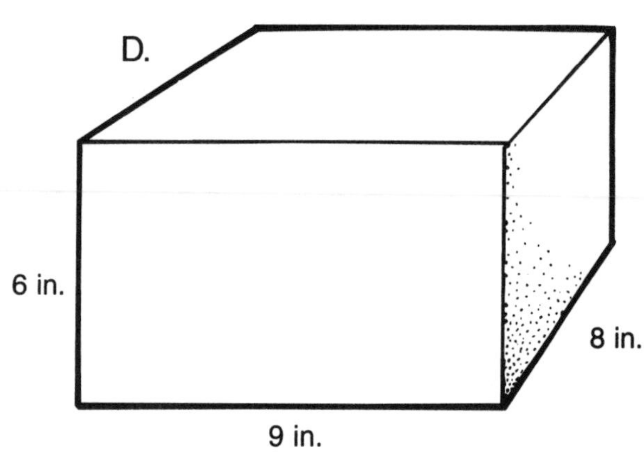

SA = __________

E.

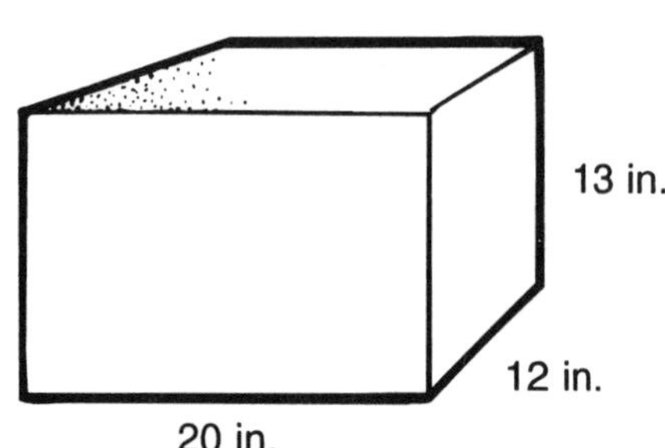

SA = __________

F.

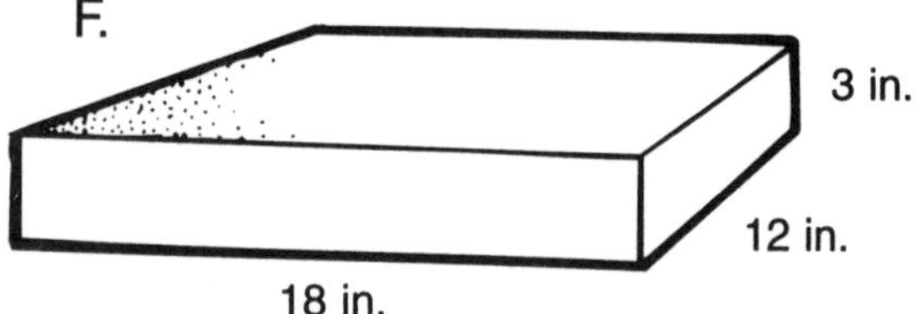

SA = __________

G.

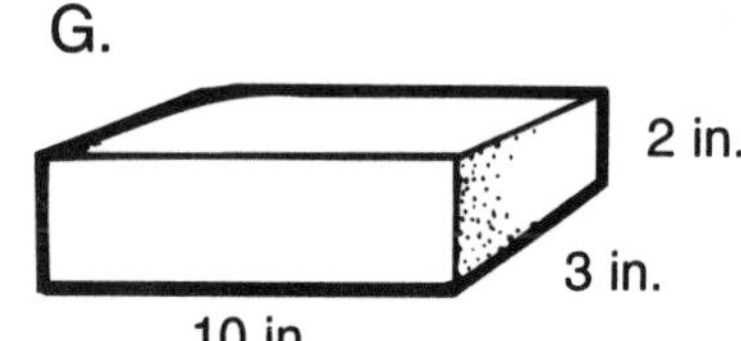

SA = __________

Name________________________________

Hold Everything!

Find the volumes below. Then cross out the sections at the bottom of the page that contain the answers. The letters in the remaining squares, written in order, will spell the answer to the following question:

Who wrote the Declaration of Independence?

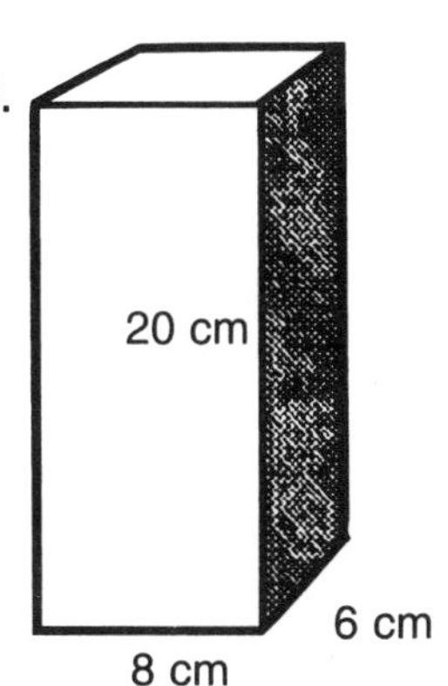

V = __________

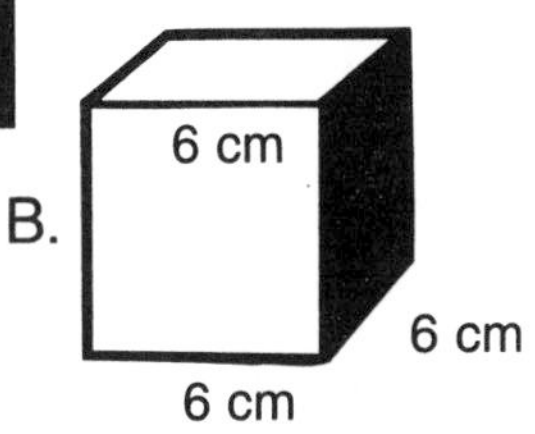

V = __________

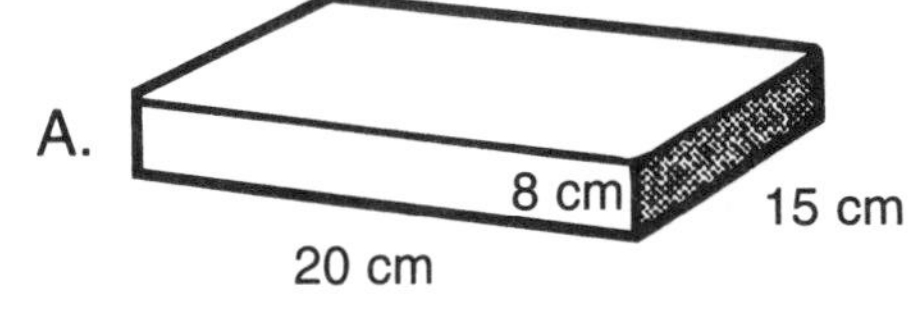

V = __________

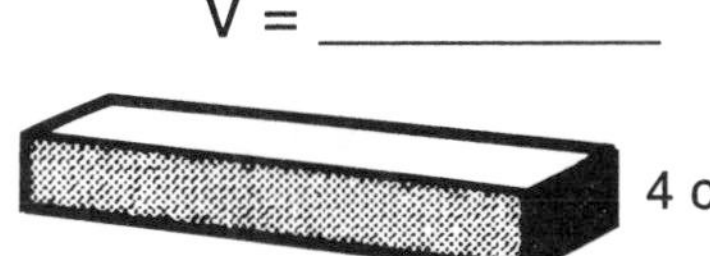

V = __________

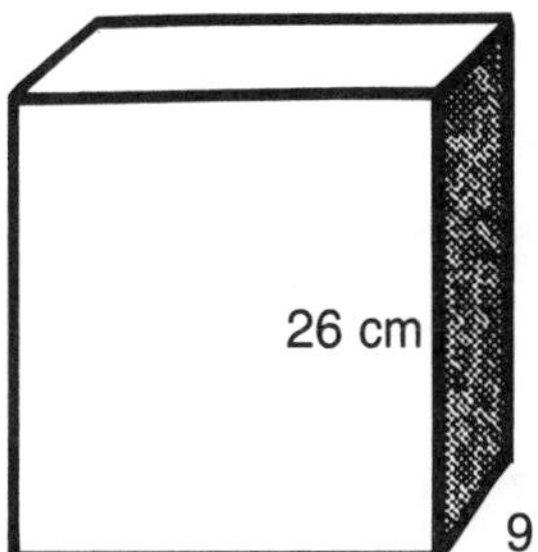

V = __________

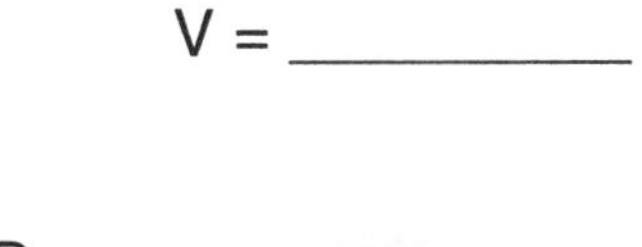

V = __________

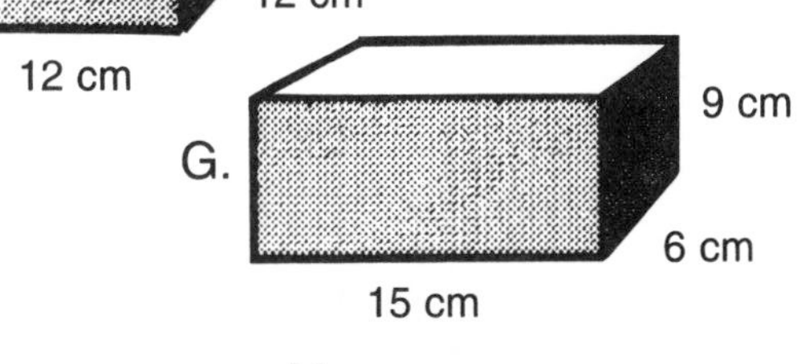

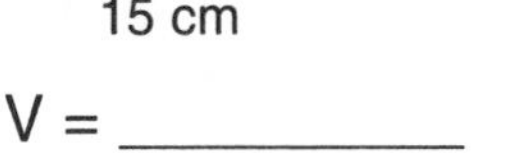

V = __________

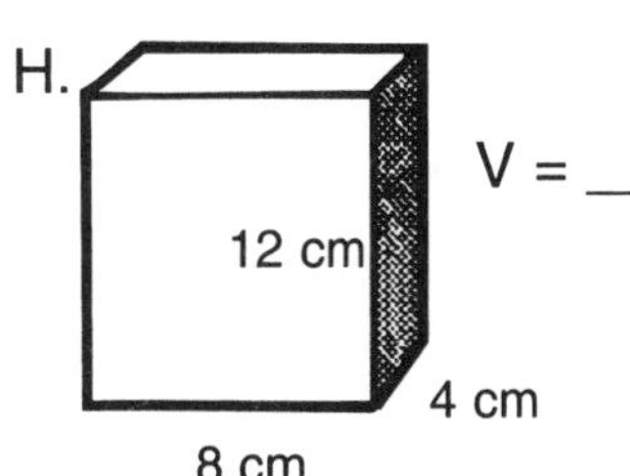

V = __________

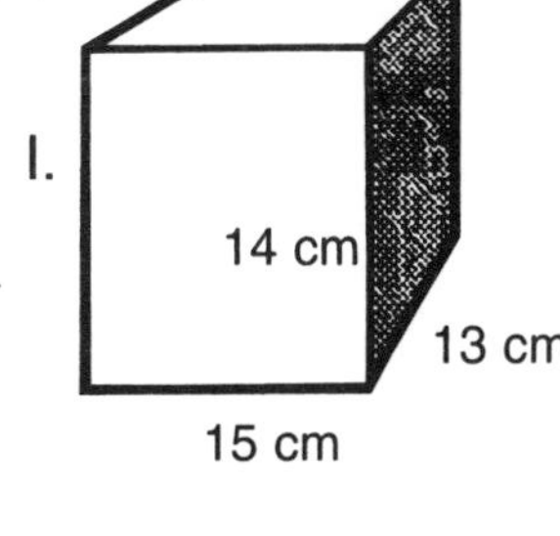

V = __________

416 cm^3 T	897 cm^3 H	810 cm^3 K	1,500 cm^3 O	216 cm^3 I	296 cm^3 M
2,930 cm^3 A	2,400 cm^3 V	246 cm^3 S	910 cm^3 J	3,456 cm^3 E	8,200 cm^3 F
1,728 cm^3 B	1,235 cm^3 F	300 cm^3 D	384 cm^3 G	9,250 cm^3 E	3,730 cm^3 R
825 cm^3 S	2,730 cm^3 L	9,340 cm^3 O	8,212 cm^3 N	4,212 cm^3 P	960 cm^3 W

___ ___ ___ ___ ___ ___   ___ ___ ___ ___ ___ ___ ___ ___ ___

Name______________________________________

Solving Real-Life Problems

Use what you know about perimeter, area, surface area, and volume to solve the problems below.

1. The Pentagon Building in Washington, D.C., has 5 equal sides. If the distance from one corner to the next is 281 meters, what is the perimeter of the building?

   ____

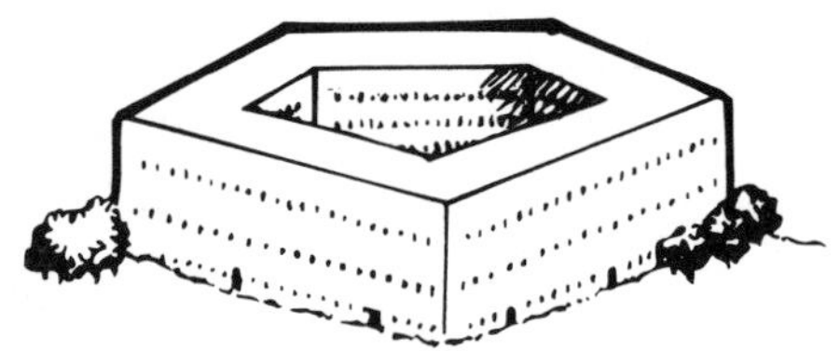

2. Andy has 50 meters of fencing for a garden. What is the greatest area he can fence in if his garden is rectangular and is a whole number of meters on each side?

   ____

3. A box is filled completely with 36 books that are 8 inches wide, 12 inches long, and 3 inches thick. What is the volume of the box?

   ____

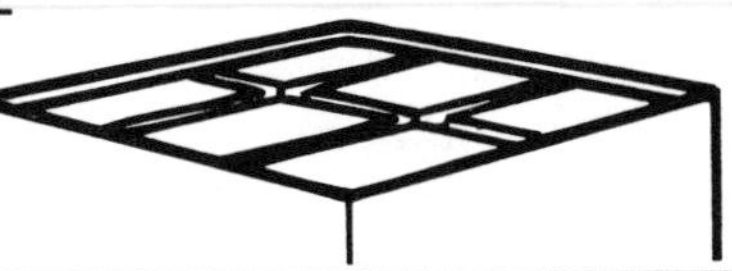

4. What would be the capacity in milliliters of an aquarium that is 40 centimeters long, 20 centimeters wide, and 30 centimeters high? (Hint: 1 cm^3 = 1 milliliter)

   ____

5. What is the least amount of wrapping paper needed to wrap a cube-shaped box with a length of 16 inches?

   ____

6. What is the surface area and volume of a cassette tape box that is 11 centimeters long, 7 centimeters wide, and 1.8 centimeters high?

   SA = ______________ V = ______________

7. You are framing a picture that is 8 inches by 10 inches. First, you plan to mat it in a 2-inch mat. (Hint: Draw a picture.)

   a. What is the perimeter of the picture? ______________

   b. What is the perimeter of the matted picture? ______________

   c. If framing is sold in 1-foot lengths for $10.95 a foot, how much will it cost to buy a frame for the matted picture? ______________

Page 4

A. 120; 140; 60; 90; 1,000
B. 100; 900; 400; 10,000; 7,000
C. 800; 500; 1,400; 600; 9,000
D. 4,000; 200; 5,000; 6,000; 18,000

The shaded sections form the word OK.

Page 5

O. 7,885 W. 3,041
N. 16,042 C. 76,540
D. 3,836 E. 4,364
K. 2,367 H. 17,531
P. 17,682 L. 2,176
U. 4,993 A. 22,210
S. 73,914 I. 11,773
F. 3,472 G. 987
T. 7,406

WHAT DOES A CHICKEN SPEAK?
FOWL LANGUAGE

Page 6

A. 762,488; 543,103; 920,064; 615,793
B. 435,784; 64,858; 900,616; 500,001
C. 514,352; 492,075; 490,247; 287,196
D. 64,039; 25,519; 138,508; 222
E.–F. Answers will vary.

Page 7

A. 8.24 B. 9.34 C. 3.79
D. 2.7 E. 9.82 F. 8.16
G. 10 H. 40.35 I. 12.11

Page 8

A. 10.8; 10.75; 5.2
B. 26.62; 3.99; 117.73
C. 4.85; 5.55; 4.22
D. 164.6; 4.419; 158.68; 75.4; 41.2
E. 7.032; 0.189; 3.94; 132.6; 5
F. 11.253; 8.65; 30.71; 803.42; 4.16
G. 34.57; 2.37; 22.019; 43.49

Page 9

1. Yes; $1.95 is about $2; $7.75 is about $8; $2 + $8 = $10
2. pie or ice cream
3. pie
4. salad and a milk shake
5. salad
6. Answers will vary.

Page 14

Possible answers:

A. 10 x 80; 20 x 40; 8 x 100
B. 10 x 100; 5 x 200; 20 x 50
C. 10 x 150; 5 x 300; 50 x 30
D. 30 x 40; 6 x 200; 60 x 20; 10 x 120
E. 80 x 200; 40 x 400; 2,000 x 8; 100 x 160
F. 50 x 400; 20 x 1,000; 100 x 200; 500 x 40
G. 10 x 400; 20 x 200; 5 x 800; 80 x 50
H. 300 x 800; 60 x 4,000; 1,200 x 200; 100 x 2,400

When turned sideways, the design shows the numerals 7 and 9.

Page 15

The following numbers should be circled in each square:

A. 5 and 39 B. 49 and 2
C. 76 and 4 D. 19 and 23
E. 21 and 43 F. 22 and 47
G. 31 and 29 H. 63 and 19
I. 29 and 52 J. 315 and 8
K. 511 and 21 L. 987 and 23

Page 16

S. 5,184 K. 2,926
A. 5,727 T. 5,625
A. 1,288 U. 2,352
S. 4,984 I. 2,304
S. 2,133 T. 2,405
R. 55,776 C. 28,388
I. 18,144 E. 42,054
O. 35,090

A SEASICK TOURIST

Page 17

A. 2.16; 0.64; 1.6; 0.72; 4.2
B. 13.3; 8.4; 26.88; 18.54; 15.64
C. 34.87; 78.26; 14.74; 76.20; 78.39
D. 5.7; 1.87; 12.3; 50.4; 8.9
E. 1.8; 78.69; 40.6; 0.78; 1.87
F. The number of decimal places in the factors and in the products is equal.

Page 18

1. 51; 510; 5,100; 51,000
2. 64.3; 643; 6,430; 64,300
3. 4.98; 498; 4,980; 49,800
4. 986; 9,860; 98,600; 986,000
5. 52.7; 527; 52,700; 527,000
6. 1,290; 12,900; 129,000; 1,290,000
7. 416; 4,160; 416,000; 4,160,000
8. 0.19; 19; 190; 1,900
9. 0.32; 3.2; 32; 320
10. 0.753; 7.53; 753; 7,530
11. 0.00034; 0.0034; 0.034; 3.4
12. 810.95; 8,109.5; 81,095; 810,950
13. Move the decimal point to the right three places to show multiplication by 1,000.

Page 19

A. 0.036; 0.19; 0.014; 0.424
B. 0.616; 4.2; 143.52; 12.516; 3.725
C. 74.218; 0.9801; 8.946; 22.269; 28.4

Alaska and Hawaii

Page 20

1. $1.05 2. $1.08 3. $2.70
4. $0.56 5. $2.40 6. $4.90
7. $0.72 8. $0.50
9. 10 minutes 10. 20 minutes

Page 21

A. 5; 4; 7
B. 10; 6; 9
C. 100; 800; 500
D. 20; 50; 70
E. 60; 30; 25
F. 80; 200; 90

THOMAS EDISON

Page 22

5	0	4		9	2	8
8		5	2	8	0	
8	4		2	9		0
8	9	6	3		3	
	5	2	4		7	9
3		7		3	9	0
3	1	2		5	2	0

Page 23

A. 0.9 (6)5.4)	0.9 (3)2.7)	B. 1.7 (8)13.6)	0.34 (4)1.36)
1.8 (6)10.8)	1.36 (9)12.2)	0.85 (8)6.8)	1.7 (4)6.8)
C. 3.6 (8)28.8)	7.2 (4)28.8)	D. 10.025 (8)80.2)	20.01 (2)40.2)
1.44 (4)5.76)	7.2 (8)57.6)	1.005 (4)4.02)	1.005 (8)8.04)
E. 2.85 (4)11.4)	2.85 (8)22.8)	F. 0.58 (8)4.64)	11.6 (4)46.4)
11.4 (2)22.8)	0.57 (2)1.14)	11.6 (2)23.2)	2.32 (4)9.28)
G. 6.2 (2)12.4)	3.1 (4)12.4)	H. 1.8 (6)10.8)	0.36 (6)2.16)
0.62 (4)2.48)	3.1 (8)24.8)	7.2 (3)21.6)	1.8 (3)5.4)

Page 24

A. $1.26 B. $29.49 C. $0.59
D. $4.60 E. $0.88 F. $0.15
G. $6.80 H. $0.09 I. $1.24

Page 25

1. 8 2. 8 3. 17
4. 16 packages; 96 buttons
5. 38 3-pair packages; 114 pairs of socks
6. yes; 4 plain uniforms

Page 28

A. 12/5 B. 17/10 C. 41/8
D. 33/5 E. 52/7 F. 22/3
G. 26/5 H. 33/8 I. 24/5
J. 13/9 K. 15/2 L. 33/12
M. 22/7 N. 29/6 O. 27/5
P. 19/4 Q. 15/8 R. 20/3
S. 29/5 T. 20/7 U. 19/6
V. 29/8 W. 19/8 X. 29/6
Y. 19/10 Z. 21/8

Page 29

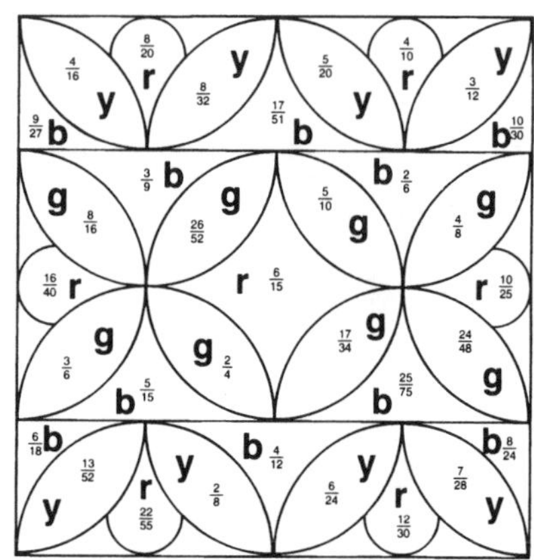

Page 30

A. 6; 4 B. 2; 1 C. 6; 3
D. 7; 2 E. 6; 7 F. 5; 12
G. 8; 18 H. 3; 6 I. 6; 9
J. 2; 16

MOUNT EVEREST

Page 31

A. 3/4; 1/5; 5/7; 1/4; 1/8
B. 5/6; 3/4; lowest terms; 2/5; 1/2
C. 1/25; 3/4; 5/12; 4/5; 8/9

Rows D & E are all in lowest terms.

F. 2/5; 9/10; 1/10; 5/6; 3/8
G. 2/5; 2/3; lowest terms; 5/6; 17/25
H. 6/7; 3/8; 1/4; 1/2; 1/3
I. 3/10; 2/3; 2/3; 1/4; 7/9

The shaded areas (lowest terms fractions) form a division sign.

Page 32

A. 2; 12; 24; 24
B. 3; 18; 54; 54
C. 5; 15; 75; 75
D. 2; 60; 120; 120
E. 3; 36; 108; 108
F. 6; 36; 216; 216
G. 2; 24; 48; 48
H. 4; 40; 160; 160
I. 3; 72; 216; 216

The product of the two factors and of the GCF and LCM is equal.

Page 33

A. 1/4, 3/8, 1/2
B. 1/3, 5/8, 3/4
C. 3/10, 1/3, 7/12
D. 2/5, 1/2, 5/8
E. 3/8, 3/5, 2/3
F. 7/12, 3/4, 4/5
G. 2/3, 5/6, 7/8
H. 5/8, 7/9, 8/9
I. 2/7, 4/9, 3/5
J. 1/2, 2/3, 3/4, 4/5
K. 2/3, 7/10, 3/4, 8/10
L. 1/4, 3/10, 3/8, 2/5
M. 3/10, 1/2, 5/12, 3/4
N. 2/3, 17/20, 9/10, 19/20

Page 38

1. 5/6 2. 1/3 3. 3/4 4. 1/2
5. 3/10 6. 3/8 7. 9/10 8. 1/2
9. 7/8 10. 7/8 11. 1/4 12. 3/4
13. 2/3 14. 5/8 15. 1/2 16. 3/4

A WRECKLESS DRIVER

Page 39

1. A. 1/8; E. 5/8; I. 1 1/8; O. 1 7/8; U. 2 5/8; L. 1 1/2; R. 2 1/4; T. 2 1/2; W. 2 7/8; M. 1 5/8; K. 1 3/8; N. 1 3/4
2. 1 3/4 3. 2 7/8 4. 3 5/8
5. 4 3/4 6. 1 5/8 7. 3 1/2
8. 6 1/8 9. 1 1/8 10. 5 1/4
11.–12. Answers will vary.

Page 40

A. 4 7/10; 5 3/8
B. 5 7/8; 8 1/2
C. 7 13/15; 9 1/4
D. 5 17/24; 8 1/10;
E. 7 7/30; 6 3/20; 10 5/14; 9 13/15
F. 5 17/20; 4 7/12; 4 1/6; 7 1/2
G. 2 7/8 + 3 3/4 + 3 3/8 = 10

Page 41

P. 5 3/8 V. 7/10 E. 3 6/35
T. 9 13/24 H. 3 1/4 E. 3 5/16
I. 2 1/2 E. 5 3/10 N. 1 1/10
D. 3 1/8 N. 2 2/15 T. 6 7/15
O. 1 7/24 H. 4 5/6 T. 5 7/8
E. 1 7/10 H. 5 1/2 E. 1/4
L. 3/4 E. 7 7/10

HE INVENTED THE TELEPHONE.

Page 42

A. (6)

1/2	4	1 1/2
3	2	1
2 1/2	0	3 1/2

B. (3)

2/5	1 2/5	1 1/5
1 4/5	1	1/5
4/5	3/5	1 3/5

C. (2 1/2)

1/2	1	1
1 1/2	3/4	1/4
1/2	3/4	1 1/4

D. (3 3/4)

2	1/4	1 1/2
3/4	1 1/4	1 3/4
1	2 1/2	1/2

E. (4 1/4)

2	1 1/2	3/4
5/8	2 3/8	1 1/4
1 5/8	3/8	2 1/4

F. (1 7/8)

1/2	3/8	1
1 1/8	5/8	1/8
1/4	7/8	3/4

Page 43

1. 8 1/4 miles 2. 9 1/8 miles
3. Least: Monday; Greatest: Friday
4. Robyn, by 3/8 mile
5. Anna, by 1/8 mile
6. Anna: about 23 miles; Robyn: about 23 miles
7. Thursday 8. Wednesday

Page 44

A. $\frac{1}{6}$ B. $\frac{3}{8}$ C. $\frac{1}{6}$
D. $\frac{1}{5}$ E. $\frac{5}{24}$ F. $\frac{2}{5}$
G. $\frac{3}{5}$ H. $\frac{1}{2}$ I. $\frac{4}{11}$
J. $\frac{1}{3}$ K. $\frac{4}{13}$ L. $\frac{2}{5}$
M. $\frac{7}{15}$ N. $\frac{25}{33}$ O. $\frac{9}{20}$

Page 45

B. $\frac{1}{56}$ H. $\frac{4}{21}$ W. $1\frac{1}{5}$
T. $\frac{10}{27}$ H. $\frac{4}{49}$ T. $3\frac{1}{3}$
H. 2 E. $\frac{8}{27}$ E. $\frac{8}{35}$
A. $\frac{1}{6}$ O. $\frac{1}{10}$ I. $\frac{3}{16}$
H. $1\frac{1}{3}$ A. $4\frac{4}{5}$ C. $\frac{1}{5}$
N. $\frac{1}{4}$ T. $\frac{2}{15}$ E. $\frac{1}{2}$
Y. $\frac{5}{36}$ A. $\frac{5}{12}$ T. $2\frac{1}{3}$
U. $\frac{4}{15}$ E. 6 S. $\frac{5}{18}$

BECAUSE HE WANTED TO HIT THE HAY

Page 46

A. $2\frac{1}{2} \times \frac{4}{5} = 2$
B. $2\frac{2}{5} \times \frac{2}{3} = 1\frac{3}{5}$
C. $1\frac{1}{2} \times 5\frac{1}{4} = 7\frac{7}{8}$
D. $\frac{3}{4} \times 2\frac{3}{4} = 2\frac{1}{6}$
E. $3\frac{1}{3} \times 2\frac{3}{4} = 9\frac{1}{6}$
F. $\frac{2}{3} \times 2\frac{1}{2} = 1\frac{2}{3}$
G. $\frac{4}{5} \times 2\frac{2}{5} = 1\frac{23}{25}$
H. $\frac{3}{4} \times 5\frac{1}{4} = 3\frac{15}{16}$
I. $2\frac{2}{5} \times 5\frac{1}{4} = 12\frac{3}{5}$
J. $2\frac{3}{4} \times 2\frac{1}{2} = 6\frac{7}{8}$
K. $2\frac{2}{5} \times 1\frac{1}{2} = 3\frac{3}{5}$
L. $3\frac{1}{3} \times 5\frac{1}{4} = 17\frac{1}{2}$
M. $\frac{2}{3} \times \frac{3}{4} = \frac{1}{2}$

Page 47

1. $2\frac{1}{2}$ cups
2. $8\frac{1}{4}$ cups
3. $1\frac{1}{3}$ cups
4. yes
5. $32\frac{1}{2}$; $6\frac{1}{4}$; $13\frac{3}{4}$; $3\frac{1}{3}$; $\frac{5}{8}$; $7\frac{1}{2}$
6. $9\frac{3}{4}$; $1\frac{7}{8}$; $4\frac{1}{8}$; 1; $\frac{3}{16}$; $2\frac{1}{4}$

Page 48

A. 3; 3 B. 2; 2
C. 2; 2 D. 3; 3
E. 12; 12 F. 10; 10
G. 1; 1 H. 6; 6
I. 4; 4 J. 8; 8
K. 1; 1 L. 12; 12
M. 30; 30 N. 24; 24
O. 24; 24

Page 51

A. $24

tennis balls	3	6	9	12	15	18
cost	$4	$8	$12	$16	$20	$24

B. 12 mugs

scoops of cocoa	5	10	15	20	25	30
mugs of hot chocolate	2	4	6	8	10	12

C. 15 minutes

quarters	2	4	6	8	10
minutes of play	3	6	9	12	15

D. 30 minutes

minutes	4	8	12	16	20	24
math problems	5	10	15	20	25	30

E. 48 markers

markers	8	16	24	32	40	48
cost	$5	$10	$15	$20	$25	$30

Page 52

A. $x = 20$; $x = 5$; $x = 45$
B. $x = 12$; $x = 15$; $x = 16$
C. $x = 18$; $x = 25$; $x = 10$
D. $x = 42$; $x = 56$; $x = 32$
E. $x = 14$; $x = 40$; $x = 63$

The UNSHADED sections will form the letter X.

Page 53

A = 11%; A = 8%; A = 17%;
A = 25%; A = 31%; E = 43%;
E = 77%; I = 49%; I = 4%;
O = 19%; O = 23%; W = 46%;
G = 25%; T = 33%; D = 79%;
T = $\frac{14}{100}$; L = $\frac{67}{100}$; M = $\frac{58}{100}$;
C = $\frac{53}{100}$; C = $\frac{28}{100}$; H = $\frac{12}{100}$;
H = $\frac{71}{100}$; N = $\frac{17}{100}$; T = $\frac{39}{100}$;
S = $\frac{84}{100}$; T = $\frac{47}{100}$; T = $\frac{75}{100}$;
D = $\frac{91}{100}$; G = $\frac{5}{100}$; L = $\frac{2}{100}$

A WATCHDOG IS A DOG THAT CAN TELL TIME.

Page 54

Page 55

1. 90%; A 2. 80%; B
3. 75%; C 4. 96%; A
5. 68%; D 6. 80%; B
7. 92%; A 8. 75%; C
9. 88%; B 10. 85%; B
11. 92%; A 12. 90%; A
13. 76%; C 14. 93%; A
15. 60%; D

Page 56

The following boxes should be crossed out:

1. $\frac{55}{100}$
2. $\frac{1}{5}$
3. 0.33
4. $\frac{5}{100}$
5. Grid shows 10%.
6. $\frac{6}{100}$
7. $\frac{3}{8}$
8. Grid shows 1%.
9. 75%

THE WINDOW

Page 59

Drawings will vary.

1. parallelogram
2. trapezoid
3. rhombus
4. rectangle
5. kite
6. square

Page 60

Answers will vary for triangles 1–4. One possible solution for each is as follows:

Triangle 1: PRM;
Triangle 2: TXY;
Triangle 3: NUW;
Triangle 4: OQV.
Triangle 5: isosceles
Triangle 6: scalene
Triangle 7: equilateral
Triangle 8: scalene
Triangle 9: isosceles

Page 61

P = 45° E = 20° W = 40°
P = 130° R = 90° E = 95°
S = 55° A = 110° A = 75°
N = 150°

A NEWSPAPER

Page 62

A. yellow, blue, red
B. red, yellow, blue
C. blue, red, yellow
D. yellow, blue, red
E. red, yellow, blue

Page 63

Answers will vary. Possible solutions include the following:

Across

1. Two figures that are the same size and shape
4. To make another figure by moving a figure without flipping or turning it
5. To turn a figure on its reverse side
6. A corner; a point that two edges have in common
9. Two rays extending from a single point
10. An angle measuring less than 90°

Down

2. An angle measuring between 90° and 180°
3. A segment that is the intersection of two faces on a figure
5. One of the surfaces making up a space (solid) figure
7. An angle measuring exactly 90°
8. Two figures that are the same shape but different size

Page 64

1. 8, 6, 14, 12
2. 6, 5, 11, 9
3. 5, 5, 10, 8
4. 10, 7, 17, 15
5. 8, 6, 14, 12
6. 6, 6, 12, 10
7. 4, 4, 8, 6

The number of edges is 2 less than the sum of the number of faces and vertices.

Page 68

A. 7.1 in. E. 3.8 in.
Y. 4.09 in. D. 4.63 in.
I. 3.35 in. R. 5.25 in.
S. 4.125 in. L. 6.2 in.

SALLY RIDE

Page 69

E. 56.52 in. R. 45.216 in.
N. 204.1 in. L. 75.36 in.
U. 125.6 in. A. 37.68 in.
A. 175.84 in. B. 50.24 in.
M. 38.308 in. L. 26.376 in.

AN UMBRELLA

Page 70

1. 108 ft.^{2}
2. 336 ft.^{2}
3. 412.5 ft.^{2}
4. 192 ft.^{2}
5. 52 ft.^{2}
6. 600 ft.^{2}
7. 9.36 ft.^{2}
8. 116.28 ft.^{2}
9. 258.3 ft.^{2}

The shaded boxes reveal the letter A.

Page 71

1. 97.5 mm^2
2. 24.5 mm^2
3. 81 mm^2
4. 11 cm^2
5. 5.88 cm^2
6. 704 mm^2
7. 256 mm^2
8. 8.775 cm^2
9. 10.08 cm^2

Page 72

A. 150 in.^{2} B. 232 in.^{2}
C. 104 in.^{2} D. 348 in.^{2}
E. 1,312 in.^{2} F. 612 in.^{2}
G. 112 in.^{2}

Page 73

A. 2,400 cm^3 B. 216 cm^3
C. 960 cm^3 D. 1,728 cm^3
E. 300 cm^3 F. 4,212 cm^3
G. 810 cm^3 H. 384 cm^3
I. 2,730 cm^3

THOMAS JEFFERSON

Page 74

1. 1,405 m
2. 12 x 13 meters; the area would be 156 m^2.
3. 10,368 in.^{3}
4. 24,000 mL
5. 1,536 in.^{2}
6. surface area = 218.8 cm^2; volume = 138.6 cm^3
7. a. 36 inches
   b. 52 inches
   c. You must buy 5 feet of frame; $54.75